El Q'anil

Volume 46

SUN TRACKS
An American Indian Literary Series

SERIES EDITOR
Ofelia Zepeda

EDITORIAL COMMITTEE
Vine Deloria, Jr.
Larry Evers
Joy Harjo
Geary Hobson
N. Scott Momaday
Irvin Morris
Simon J. Ortiz
Emory Sekaquaptewa
Kate Shanley
Leslie Marmon Silko
Luci Tapahonso

El Q'anil:
Man of Lightning

A legend of Jacaltenango, Guatemala,
in English, Spanish, and Popb'al Ti'
(Jakaltek Maya)

VÍCTOR D. MONTEJO

English translation by
WALLACE KAUFMAN & SUSAN G. RASCÓN

The University of Arizona Press   Tucson

First Printing
The University of Arizona Press
© 2001 Víctor D. Montejo

⊖ This book is printed on acid-free, archival-quality paper.
Manufactured in the United States of America

06   05   04   03   02   01   6   5   4   3   2   1

Library of Congress Cataloging-in-Publication Data
Montejo, Victor, 1951–
[Kanil, man of lightning. Polyglot]
El Q'anil : man of lightning / Victor D. Montejo ; English
translation by Wallace Kaufman and Susan G. Rascón.
p.   cm. — (Sun tracks ; v. 46)
Includes bibliographical references.
ISBN 0-8165-2082-8 (acid-free paper)
1. Jacalteca Indians—Folklore   2. Legends—Guatemala—
Jacaltenango.   3. Jacalteca language—Texts.   I. Kaufman,
Wallace, 1951–   II. Rascón, Susan Giersbach.
III. Title.   IV. Series.
PS501 .S85 vol. 46
[F1465.2.J3]
810.8'0054 s—dc21   [398.2/089   00-009431

British Library Cataloguing-in-Publication Data
A catalogue record for this book is available from the British Library.

I dedicate this book to my brother, Pedro Antonio Montejo, of blessed memory. He encouraged me to write the stories of our people and to listen to the voices of the elders.

I also dedicate this book to Antun Luk, of blessed memory. This elder and friend taught me to value and revitalize my Jakaltek Maya cultural heritage.

The University of Arizona Press

520-621-1441 Fax: 520-621-8899 355 S. Euclid Ave. 103, Tucson, AZ 85719

NOTE NEW ADDRESS
355 S. Euclid Ste. 103
Tucson, AZ 85701

Classic Mayan legend, preserved in trilingual edition by Mayan author Victor Montejo

El Q'anil: Man of Lightning

Popb'al Ti (Jakaltek Maya), English, and Spanish

###

El Q'anil: Man of Lightning, Popb'al Ti (Jakaltek Maya), English, and Spanish is available May 2001.

Classic Mayan legend in Popb'al Ti (Jakaltek Maya) and Spanish by Wallace Kaufman and Susan G. Rascón. His reconstruction

Contents

Foreword

In August of 1980 my ten-year-old daughter and I sat with seventy campesinos crammed onto and between the seats of an overworked bus that roared and coughed its slow way through the mountains of northern Guatemala. People squatting in the aisle wedged a short, broad-shouldered Maya against us. For their own security, Guatemala's Mayas talk little in public and less to strangers. *"Los orejas,"* "the ears" (or spies), of the people who kill, can hear anything and are always ready to make the worst of it. Pedro Antonio, the young man next to us, refused to live in that prison of silence. He told us about himself and about his brother Víctor Dionicio, who wrote stories and collected the old Maya legends.

Six months later when I arrived to visit Pedro Antonio and the brother of whom he was so proud, a telegram met me in Huehuetenango, the provincial capital. "Pedro Antonio passed away tragically yesterday." At that time to say much more would have been dangerous. Pedro Antonio had been shot down by five soldiers in the town square during a fiesta. The next day he would have started teaching adults raised in an oral culture how to read and write.

I did not go to Jacaltenango to see the grieving family I had never met. I sent a telegram and a little money. As I traveled around Guatemala, I wondered about Pedro Antonio's brother. How and why would a young man stay put in the midst of civil war to teach children, listen to old people retell stories of long-dead Mayas, and, night after night, write the history of this little corner of the world?

When I returned to the United States, my telegram and gift were answered by a letter from Víctor. Later, he began sending fiction, poetry, and some legends and fables. His is the work of someone who belongs to a people and a place and a heritage as clearly as a limb grows from a tree.

It has become fashionable recently for educated Americans to search nostalgically for roots from which they were severed long ago. Some write books in which, traveling like visitors encased in a time machine, they visit the people and places of their supposed ancestors. Víctor Montejo is an educated man whose roots are alive in his land and his people. He knows, however, that these people are few and their lands small. Thousands of them have fled to Mexico, where they are refugees.

Their culture cannot always go with them. If they sell their weaving, they are competing with Mexicans for tourist money. If they wear their native clothes outside the refugee camps or even speak in their accented Spanish, they can be identified as refugees and deported to Guatemala, where someone might assume that in their absence they have been with the guerrillas.

Contrary to the claims of some people who like their pathos simple and ultimate, the war in Guatemala is not genocide aimed at eradicating the Mayas. Tens of thousands have died. Their deaths are a great crime but certainly not the end of the country's more than five million *indígenas*. If we see only those gruesome deaths, we will miss something equally important. Their obvious deaths are the signs of a much larger form of dying—the dying of Maya culture as a result of violence.

Maybe it won't happen. Maybe Guatemala will find a way to unite its Maya majority and its ladino and white criollo minorities in peace. Meanwhile, Víctor Montejo is like a highly trained space traveler carrying living fragments of his culture to alien worlds. We know of others throughout history: Aesop, Homer, the survivors of Russian pogroms, Garcilaso the Inca, a handful of Native Americans. Many anthropologists, travelers, and novelists have used indigenous material from Latin America. Some have lived close to or among indigenous people. Some have indigenous forebears a few generations back. The indígena who speaks out of the midst of the culture in its own voice and consciousness is very rare.

The reasons are many. Most are poor. Most do not read or write. Indigenous centers survive because they are far from literary centers, publishing houses, and bookstores. Schools are crude, and libraries nonexistent. The few parents who think their children might become something besides laborers urge them to be clerks, teachers, maybe lawyers or politicians— not writers.

One evening on Víctor's first visit to the United States, the talk among the little group of people turned to our childhood and what we had expected to be when we grew up. I asked Víctor. At first he thought he didn't understand the question. When I explained how children in the United States think about their adult careers, he looked amused. "I always knew what I would be. I would work the fields like my father," he said.

When he was six years old, he begged his father to let him attend a new Maryknoll boarding school in Jacaltenango, a regional market center, some twenty-four kilometers from their village. At the beginning of each month, his father came to see him at the boarding school, with a mule loaded with a bag of corn on one side and firewood on the other. That was the beginning of the education that would allow Víctor Montejo to become a voice for his people beyond the Cuchumatán Mountains. His teachers had to convince him to follow his dreams of attending middle school. And teachers there found him a scholarship to attend a seminary and then an institute that trained indigenous teachers.

School was not his only education. Before he ever entered a classroom, his education had begun with stories told and retold by his mother, his grandparents, and village elders. His grandfather had been a community leader. His mother has an oral memory that preserves stories in great detail year after year.

Víctor's education carried him out of the mountains to a seminary in Sololá and a vocational school in the old colonial capital of Antigua Guatemala. The farther he got from Jacaltenango, the more he realized the uniqueness and value of his own culture. He began writing about his people and recording the legends and fables he knew, not because he wanted to be a writer, but because he did not want the past to disappear.

He became a certified urban teacher, but Indians seldom get to teach in urban schools populated by ladinos. Back in the mountains he began to seek out the old people who knew the legends. He carefully pieced together whole stories from bits and pieces. He began to write them in a Spanish that was faithful to the facts and that captured the flow and dignity of the Maya storyteller.

It is fitting that Víctor Montejo's first publication is the story most central to his people, some 35,000 remaining Jakalteks. A few crude fragments of the story were recorded by Oliver La Farge in 1927, working with the Tulane University studies in Central America. In *The Year Bearer's People* (La Farge and Byers 1931), La Farge recognized Jacaltenango's unique preservation of old Maya culture. He lamented that his "informants" were often shy and their stories incomplete and that he did not understand their language well. The storytellers then as always did not trust outsiders with their heritage.

We are fortunate now that one of the Year Bearer's people has gathered together the pieces of the story of El Q'anil, written it as he knows it should be written, and offered it to us.

WALLACE KAUFMAN

Acknowledgments

I would like to thank all those friends and colleagues who have made the publication of this book possible. In the first place, my parents Eusebio Montejo and Juana E. Méndez, who told me the story of Q'anil when I was a child; the elderly storytellers in my village, especially Antun Luk, of blessed memory; and all the Jakalteks who appreciate the work of cultural recovery I am carrying out.

I would like to thank Wallace Kaufman, who invited me to the United States in 1982 to help him translate *El Q'anil* into English. This invitation gave me the opportunity to leave Guatemala, where my life was in danger because of the violence that gripped the country in the 1980s. I also would like to thank LaVonne Poteet for promoting the use of the English-Spanish version of the book in her literature and folklore classes, and Judith Thorn, who has also used the book in her literature and folklore classes. Thanks to my translator, Susan Giersbach Rascón, who has done an excellent job of refining the English text that appears in this edition. Finally, I would like to thank Dr. Fernando Peñalosa, good friend and excellent publisher and editor, who has assisted me in preparing this manuscript for publication; and at the University of Arizona Press, Patti Hartmann and the anonymous reviewers who recommended the publication of this trilingual edition.

Introduction

The town of Jacaltenango, unknown to the world and even to many Guatemalans, is set in the backyard of the Cuchumatán Mountains in western Guatemala, where the Blue River springs forth, shining, from within the earth, nourishing everything along its course.

Despite the rapid changes of this century and the waves of political violence that have severely shaken the indigenous communities in Guatemala, the Jakalteks keep alive some of the most important characteristics of their ancestral culture. These translate today into acts of unity, respect, and mutual aid among the inhabitants of the home of the *k'uh winaj,* the "Men of Lightning," whose hero is Xhuwan Q'anil.

Xhuwan Q'anil was the man known as Juan Mendoza. His story, preserved in the oral tradition, has come down to us through the generations and constitutes part of the very essence of each and every Jakaltek.

The origins of the Jakalteks, like those of other indigenous peoples of Guatemala, have been lost in the rise and fall of the Maya. What remains is their living language, in which the story of Xhuwan Q'anil has been faithfully preserved. It is not simply a story but rather a model of virtues that portrays the thoughts and feelings of the Jakalteks over time.

In this age of space travel and possible nuclear war, it is surprising to see that Jakaltek elders still climb to the peak of Mount Q'anil to burn copal and black tallow candles, praying to Komam Yahaw Satkanh, the lord of the sky, for Q'anil's protection of the children of Jacaltenango. This ceremony occurs especially when young men are conscripted for military service and when there are reports of imminent war. The prayer is directed to Komam Q'anil (Father Q'anil), who is now personified in Xhuwan Q'anil, because the ancestors believed that "in wartime a Q'anil [Man of Lightning] lives in each and every Jakaltek." This story, then, has been the focal point of one of the most important ceremonies in Jacaltenango and southern Chiapas, Mexico.

The legend tells that our protector, the Man of Lightning, always walks before the sons of Jacaltenango and protects them, destroying all dangers and obstacles in their path. Such is the case with the group of Jakalteks in this narrative, who returned victorious from an extremely important mission across the sea. Our elders declare that after such a dangerous journey, every Jakaltek must return to his homeland to be united with his people; he must not become separated from the rest.

The first Q'anil (and now Xhuwan Q'anil) referred to one of the four Year Bearers who, according to our ancient calendar, succeed each other in this order: Q'anil, Watanh, Ah, and Chinax. Q'anil is a more humanitarian patron of war, chosen by our ancestors over the bloodthirsty Tojil of other peoples who, according to the *Popol Wuj,* came from the East.

Jakaltek elders, such as octogenarian Antun Luk, who preserved the culture and oral tradition and wore the traditional dress of Jacaltenango, have told me this story, which they do not set in a particular time or place. Part of the story or legend may refer to pre-Hispanic times and part to events that occurred during the Spanish conquest itself. In Maya oral tradition, the storytellers keep oral histories alive, adapting them to new historical situations. Similarly, the crossing of the sea is always mentioned in ethnohistorical sources such as the *Popol Wuj* and the *Annals of the Kaqchikels.* Such is the case with *El Q'anil,* in which the storytellers mention that our Jakaltek heroes went to a war "far away, across the sea."

This legend is part of the life experience of the Jakaltek people. It could be said that if this story disappears, many aspects of our culture will also disappear, as has begun to happen with the tragedies of the twentieth century, especially in the indigenous communities, where many of the languages, traditional dress, dances, music, and other traditions are being lost.

The Jakaltek Maya nation is a tiny percentage of the millions of inhabitants of Guatemala. In recent years many have had to flee the terror of widespread political violence in the country. Therefore, this has been a very difficult time to speak of the pride and dignity of indigenous peoples.

Knowing this, I have nevertheless compiled this important story from the treasure trove of our elders' memories before it disappears and shared it with the outside world. The story of Q'anil represents a cultural contribution of the Jakaltek people, worthy of being counted among the most remarkable tales in human history. And in order that we, too, in our daily labors, may value the cultural and spiritual legacy of the Maya, I offer the legend of Xhuwan Q'anil, the man who chose to abandon his family and his homeland and to offer up his own life for the freedom of his people—an admirable gesture that lives on in the marvelous traditions of the Jakaltek Maya people.

El Q'anil in Maya Oral and Written Tradition

Oral tradition is an extraordinary vein of literary richness that is maintained, lost, or transformed in the daily speech of the indigenous people of Guatemala. From this oral tradition have come several native ethnohistorical and literary documents that have warranted the attention of national and foreign scholars. Some of these documents are the *Popol Wuj, Annals of the Kaqchikels, Title of the Lords of Totonicapán, Rabinal Achí,* and the *Books of Chilam Balam.* Compared with the importance ascribed to these documents, less attention has been paid to the indigenous literature maintained in the oral tradition, which has been considered merely a quaint expression of a disappeared past. In reality, the oral traditions of the present-day Maya peoples are also of great importance, because their content expresses dramatic moments that the Maya peoples have experienced throughout their history. Despite the denial by non-Mayas of these values and of the indigenous system of knowledge, the Maya continued to express their creative and philosophical thought through stories, fables, legends, and histories, which live on in the oral tradition of the modern Maya peoples.

Several specialists and translators of such ethnohistorical documents as the *Popol Wuj, Annals of the Kaqchikels,* and the *Chilam Balam* believe that parts of those documents were written in hieroglyphics in pre-Hispanic times.[1] In other words, the Maya had a written (hieroglyphic) literary tradition, which has come down to us in fragments through the oral tradition.

Unfortunately, the wars of conquest destroyed the native documents that contained the ancient histories and other knowledge of these native peoples of America. We have, for example, the case of the book-burning in Yucatán by Bishop Diego de Landa. In his *Relación de las cosas de Yucatán* (1983), Landa refers to the destruction of the Maya books and codices: "These people also used certain characters or letters with which they wrote their ancient things and their sciences in their books, and with these figures and some signs of the same, they understood their things and made them understood and taught. We found a great number of books of these letters of theirs, and because there was nothing in them but superstition and falsehood of the devil, we burned them all, at which they felt astonished and were very sad." (Landa 1983:117–18)

Some years after this tragedy, the missionaries themselves, along with indigenous people who had learned to read and write in Spanish, devoted themselves to salvaging what they could of the oral tradition, which was being lost with the invasion and Spanish colonization.

In the region of the Cuchumatán Mountains, the recovery of native documents of the quality of the aforementioned indigenous books has been poor. The region has been too neglected in terms of cultural recovery during the colonial period and even up to the present day. Each Maya linguistic community has maintained or re-created its own particular culture (all of them derived from one common trunk, Maya), but not all have had the same good fortune in preserving their documents. For example, in the early 1940s, Catholic missionaries arrived in the Cuchumatán communities and used Landa's method of flogging and imprisoning the *alkal txah* (*alcaldes rezadores* or sacred officials[2]) and the *ahb'e* (Maya calendar experts and diviners) to make them abandon their religious practices. The burning of the ancient books was an act of brutality performed not only by the missionaries and invaders of the past. This tragedy of erasing the histories of the indigenous peoples has been repeated often in modern times as well. For example, the elders tell of an incident of book burning outside the town hall of Jacaltenango in the early 1950s. The elders state that every year they would take out the ancient books, which were covered in deerskin, and would, because of the humidity, dry them on straw mats outside the municipal building. But when the ladinoized indigenous people occupied the positions of authority in the community (1940–1960), the Year Bearer ceremony (Ijom Hab'il), which Oliver La Farge had described a few years earlier in his ethnography *The Year Bearer's People* (1931), ceased to be celebrated. The new city mayors, who cancelled the traditional positions of alcaldes rezadores, decided to burn the ancient books, which were kept in the Royal Coffer. Keeping them, in their view, was tantamount to continuing to believe in the "superstitions" of the ancestors. Some of the registries of baptisms, marriages, and colonial tributes are held today in the museum of the Jacaltenango Hospital, thanks to the concern of Dr. Dorothy Erickson (Sister Rose), a Maryknoll missionary, and Father Arnulfo Delgado, who saw to preserving the documents (Cox de Collins 1980; Lovell 1992a).

In other places, the destruction of ancient documents was the result of vandalism by ladinos who did not understand the historical, religious, and cultural value of such documents for the indigenous people. Maud Oakes renders this account of the destruction of some ancient books in Todos Santos Cuchumatanes: "One time, many years ago, I am told, when the Intendente was a ladino, the Indians were carrying the Caja Real in a procession. Some drunk ladinos attacked the procession and broke open the Caja Real. I am told that in it they found some old deeds and other papers and a long roll of skin with colored figures on it." (Oakes 1951:66)

In general terms, we have very little knowledge of the written indigenous literature in the Cuchumatán Mountains because ethnohistorical documents such as the *Popol Wuj, Chilam Balam,* and *Annals of the Kaqchikels* have not survived in the region. What is currently known are the ethnographic reports of modern anthropologists and researchers who studied the region during the first half of the 1900s. In the particular case of Jacaltenango, we have the ethnographies of La Farge and Byers's *The Year Bearer's People* (1931, 1997) and La Farge's *Santa Eulalia: The Religion of a Cuchumatán Indian Town* (1947, 1994), which are important for understanding the religion, calendar, and folklore of the Jakaltek and Q'anjob'al Maya. When speaking of Maya literature, attention is turned immediately to the *Popol Wuj* of the K'iche' or the *Books of the Chilam Balam* of the Yukateks. The reason is clear: These are monumental works that have survived to the present day and that were written with Latin characters by the indigenous people themselves shortly after the Spanish invasion. In reality, many of these historical accounts have continued to be transmitted orally from one generation to the next, although it must be recognized that many have gradually been lost, transformed, or re-created over time. In addition, many of the elderly storytellers have died, and the oral tradition has lost some of the power and importance that it had at the beginning of the century.

I will now discuss the oral literature of the Jakaltek Maya of Northwestern Guatemala, and especially the legend of El Q'anil, "The Man of Lightning." In the process, I will explain how El Q'anil has reached us today and how I interwove different short versions of the legend in order to construct and create the text presented here.

The Man of Lightning in Historical Accounts

The *Popol Wuj* has been the ethnohistorical book par excellence, as it has been translated into many languages. In this book one can observe the force of thunder and lightning in the creation of the world according to the stories of the Maya-K'iche'. At the beginning of the narration, the Creator and Former, called "Heart of the Sky," was in darkness and manifested himself in three forms: "[T]hey conceived the growth, the generation of trees, of bushes, and the growth of life, of humankind, in the blackness, in the early dawn, all because of the Heart of the Sky, named Hurricane. Thunderbolt Hurricane comes first, the second is Newborn Thunderbolt, and the third is Sudden Thunderbolt. So there were three of them, as Heart of the Sky" (Tedlock 1996:65).

According to Father Ximénez, who did the original translation of the manuscript of Chichicastenango, "Kakulja Juraqan" translates as "bolt of a leg or lightning," Chipi Kakulja is "small lightning bolt," and Raxa Kakulja is "green lightning bolt."[2] Unlike the *Popol Wuj* and the other Maya books that were discovered by chance by their translators in the Mayan languages, *El Q'anil* has survived in the oral tradition of the people of Jacaltenango over the centuries, though with the changes and transformations characteristic of the oral tradition. The name "Q'anil" is itself an ancient Maya name and one of the four Year Bearers (Q'anil, Watanh, Ah, and Chinax), according to the Jakaltek Maya calendar. Additionally, Q'anil was one of the first ancestors and founders of the town of Xajla' (Jacalte-nango), according to ancient Jakaltek traditions and cosmogony. Thus, in the *Título de Jacaltenango,* brought to light by Agustín Estrada Monroy, the name "Juan Canil" (Xhuwan Q'anil) is mentioned:

> We principals of this town of Jacaltenango saw and understood the words of the elders Our Ancestors named Tomás Juárez, Domingo Graviel, Don Bernabé Domingo, Lorenzo de Vargas, what it is that their Parents and those said to them what the beginning of Our Natural Lord who is called Quesea Ajau, which means Natural Lord, was like . . . and he left an order to a brother of theirs, Juan Canil, and another brother of his, Jun Yc, and to his brother Hun Canil he left power, in order that he could travel the land to see what was of best disposition to give them sustenance cultivating it. (Estrada Monroy 1985:291)

According to what is mentioned in this excerpt, the original *Title of Jacaltenango* was written in a Mexican language (Náhuatl), but its where-abouts was unknown. In terms of the written history of Jacaltenango, this is the oldest-known text, and in it is recorded in writing the complete name Juan Canil, or Xhuwan Q'anil, as one of the founding fathers of the town, although the name "Juan" (Xhuwan) is a common name for heroes in the mythical accounts of the Maya (Pickands 1986).

Later, in the account (also a lost document) of the invasion of the Cuchumatanes by Gonzalo de Alvarado, mention is made of a great military chief of K'aib'il B'alam, whose name is Q'anil Akab'. According to the *Recordación Florida* of Fuentes y Guzmán (1969–1972), the Mams and their allies, which included the Jakalteks, went to confront the invaders in Malacatancito on the outskirts of Chinab'ul (Huehuetenango). "The Malakateks fought valiantly, but when their chief Canil Acab was killed by the lance of Gonzalo de Alvarado, their courage quickly declined" (Lovell 1985:61).

Then, when Pedro de Alvarado enslaved his allies, the Kaqchikels, to wash gold in Pankán, there is an account of the presence of a "man of lightning" in the *Annals of the Kaqchikels.* According to this indigenous document, a man of lightning, or "demon" as they called him, arrived to offer his help to liberate the Kaqchikels from slavery and the demand for tribute to which they were subjected by Tunatiu (Alvarado). With his characteristic cruelty, Alvarado was willing to destroy the Kaqchikels if they did not obey his orders: "Get the metal and bring it within five days. Woe to you if you do not bring it! I know my heart!" (Recinos 1980:128). Upon seeing the suffering of this people, ". . . a man, an agent of the devil, appeared and said to the kings: 'I am the lightning. I will kill the Spaniards; by fire they shall perish. When I strike the drum, depart [everyone] from the city; let the lords go to the other side of the river. This I will do on the day 7 Ahmak [August 26, 1524].' Thus that demon spoke to the lords." (Recinos 1980:129)[3]

From the fact that a man of lightning or demon is mentioned in the *Annals of the Kaqchikels,* we can infer that in pre-Hispanic times the belief in the man of lightning existed in Maya culture. This legendary mythical character is characterized by his sacrifice and self-denial as he appears in defense of the oppressed. In the same way, we can note the similarity between the role of Xhuwan Q'anil and his helper and that of the twin heroes in the *Popol Wuj,* who had to pass tests and return as conquerors of Xibalba, as recounted by Pickands: "They undergo magical trials, then perform an act which transforms them into spirit-beings of great power. They totally destroy the people of the faraway place, using magical weapons, but accept a plea for mercy by the enemy king and come to terms with him. They are rewarded and return home" (Pickands 1986:103).

This is the process seen in the story of Xhuwan Q'anil and the other men of lightning who appeared in defense of the town that was being destroyed by invading forces that fought from the sea.

Other ethnohistorical documents give accounts of the transformation of some indigenous captains into lightning bolts in order to defeat Pedro de Alvarado during the Spanish conquest of Guatemala. For example, the Maya-K'iche' vision of the Spanish conquest and the presence of men of lightning in combat is related vividly in the *Titles of the House of Nehaib:*

> The indigenous people who could not kill Tunatiu and the lady that protected them returned and again sent another captain who was capable of changing into a lightning bolt, whose name was Izquin Ahpalotz Utzakibalha, also called Nehaib. And this Nehaib went to confront the Spaniards as a lightning bolt, desiring to kill the Gover-

nor, but as he approached, he immediately saw above the Spaniards an extremely white dove, which was protecting them. He returned again, but immediately was blinded, falling to the ground unable to get up. Three times this captain transformed into a lightning bolt charged against the Spaniards, and three times he was thrown to the ground when his eyes were blinded. (Recinos 1983:86–90)

Similarly, among the Tzotzils and Tzeltals of Chiapas, Mexico, there also existed the idea of defending oneself against the Spaniards using magical and powerful weapons, such as the lightning bolt. Later, during the Tzotzil and Tzeltal uprising of 1712, four women met to invoke supernatural powers to defeat the enemy, who used powerful weapons. "Each woman represented a natural force: earthquake, lightning, flood, and wind. They planned to hurl lightning at Cosío, whip up floods that would inundate the Spaniards, and cause earthquakes that would bury the Spaniards beneath their rubble" (Bricker 1981:64).

But according to the testimonies and accusations against the participants in that colonial rebellion, the efforts of these women also failed: "They were unable to unleash these supernatural forces to defeat the Spaniards" (Bricker 1981:64).

Among the Yukateks exists the legend of Don Antonio Martínez, who fought the enemy from Havana, according to the *Chilam Balam*. The enemy fought from the sea in thirteen boats, and Don Antonio Martínez utilized supernatural powers to defeat them: "'Let nine chairs be raised up for us to sit on. The sea shall burn. I shall be raised up.' There was fire in his eye. 'Sand and spray shall be raised aloft. The face of the sun shall be darkened by the great tempest.' Whereupon the captain accoutered himself. '[Everything] shall be blown to the ground by the wind. In the meantime I sit on my chair'; in the meantime the fleet of thirteen ships comes" (Roys 1967:124).

The man of lightning is omnipresent in Jakaltek stories and oral tradition, although he is also a character that figures (though to a lesser degree) in the present-day oral tradition of other Maya peoples of the Mesoamerican region. For example, in the ethnic conflicts that existed between the Tojolabals of Margaritas, Chiapas, Mexico, and their neighbors, the Chujes of Guatemala, confrontations between the men of lightning of both Maya groups are mentioned. The wars between the two peoples, according to oral tradition, were caused by a struggle for control of the salt mines, which are found in Chuj territory. The Tojolabal elders say the following about these wars between Chuj and Tojolabal men of lightning:

> They gathered where the fight of lightning bolts against lightning bolts was going to be held. The opponents, when they saw them coming, formed a cloud that came from the jungle and moved toward the place where the fight was going to be. When the cloud arrived, it began to unleash lightning bolts and very strong winds, and they say that where the wind blew, it uprooted all the trees, broke them to pieces, and cast them far away. The other lightning bolts said: "Well, they have demonstrated their strength, they are powerful and strong. Now we are going to show them ours and we'll see what happens." They began to unleash their lightning bolts and, without their opponents realizing it, they took advantage of the opportunity to take the soul from their land. The other lightning bolts were busy fighting and did not realize how they took it from them; when they realized what had happened it was already too late. They were defeated, and returned to the place from which they had come. (Lomelí González 1988:35–36)

Among many indigenous groups in Guatemala, the lightning bolt plays a part in their myth regarding the discovery of corn. The *Popol Wuj* does not mention the lightning bolt that helps to break open the mountain where the seeds are kept, but the oral tradition of other Maya peoples mentions the assistance provided by the lightning in the discovery of corn. Among the Jakalteks, the lightning helps to break the stone of K'unha Ch'en (the Sacred House of Stone or granary of stone) to enable them to remove the corn. Therefrom is born the story of the different colors or types of corn. The corn that was burned by the lightning acquired a black color, the corn that was touched but not burned acquired a yellow color, and the corn that was not touched by the lightning was the white corn. This legend of the discovery of corn and the participation of the lightning in this event is common among many of the Maya peoples, such as the Mams, Tojolabals, Chujes, and Q'anjob'als.

Among other Maya peoples, the lightning is also considered a guardian angel. Among the Ixils, it is believed that "those who cause the lightning and those who provoke the thunder are angels, but previously they were people, or human beings" (Colby and Colby 1981:167). Among the Mopans, Q'eqchi's, and Achi's, thunder is produced by volcanoes or by the weapons (rifles) of the guardian angels when they fire at snakes and make dangers disappear (Shaw 1971:26–27). The Q'eqchi's and the Ixils believe that a woman who runs off with her lover can be struck by lightning. The legend of María Markaao among the Ixils is a good example. María Markaao, daughter of the god Mataqtani, permits a hummingbird to enter her room; when she closes the door, the hummingbird changes into a man, her lover Oyew Achi. The father of the young woman becomes angry and locks them in an *ika* (steam bath), but the lovers are assisted by a mole, who digs a tunnel under the ground, and in this way they escape. Then they arrive at a very narrow hole through which Oyew Achi passes, but María Markaao gets stuck because she is very fat. The father finds them and strikes his trapped daughter with lightning. Oyew Achi gathers up María's bones and takes them to his house, putting them away in an urn. Then he asks his aunt not to open the urn, because he is going away. Several days later, a noise begins to come from inside the urn, arousing the curiosity of the aunt, who opens the urn to examine its contents. At that moment, animals of many species rush out of the urn and flee toward the forest. These include deer, rabbits, squirrels, wild boars, and many others; from those bones come the animals known in the Maya region (Colby and Colby 1981:180–83).

As mentioned previously, the man of lightning is a character found in the mythology of many peoples of the Mesoamerican region. Among the Mixes of Oaxaca, the lightning bolt is a principal agent in the oral tradition. According to the Mixes's belief, men and women can have the lightning bolt as their "tonal" or alter ego. According to Spero (1987), there are two types of lightning. The greater lightning bolts were ancestors or persons who lived in the past and who are now incorporated into the supernatural world. These greater lightning bolts are considered ancestors and protectors of the people. "The lesser lightning bolts are also supernatural, but can change form, and often appear as serpents" (Spero 1987:19).

The man of lightning in the oral tradition of the Popolucas of Veracruz also resembles that of the Jakalteks, although the scene (the underworld) of the battles of the greater lightning bolt, Homxuk (Lord Lightning), is similar to that of the hero twins in the *Popol Wuj*.

El Q'anil: From Oral Tradition to Written Text

My interest in writing the Jakaltek oral tradition came about gradually. While I was studying to be an elementary schoolteacher at the Instituto Indígena para Varones "Santiago" in Antigua, Guatemala (1970–1972), I carefully read the *Popol Wuj* and the *Annals of the Kaqchikels*. These books opened the door for me to become more familiar with the written histories of the Maya of Guatemala after the Spanish invasion in 1524. At the same time, these literary jewels made me reflect on the value of the unwritten literature of the Cuchumatán Mountains region, which was slowly disappearing. Perhaps in the past a *Popol Wuj* also existed among the Jakalteks, because in ancient times the great cultural centers like Niman Konhob' (Jacaltenango) had their own sacred books, known as *popb'al hum*, in the Popb'al Ti' (Jakaltek) Maya language. Unfortunately, much of Jakaltek oral tradition has been lost, and we the descendants lament this loss. The legend of *El Q'anil: Man of Lightning* has remained, though with the changes and transformations common to oral tradition. In 1929, La Farge had difficulty obtaining the excerpts of *El Q'anil* published in *The Year Bearer's People* (La Farge and Byers, 1931). Referring to this fragmentation of the story and the distrust of the elders in telling the legend of *El Q'anil* to foreigners, La Farge tells us: "Shuwan Manel admitted frankly that he was afraid to tell it to us for fear of its hero, who today inhabits the big hill that dominates the western view. Other informants would hurry through it or tell only some fragment" (La Farge and Byers 1931:118–19).

In my case, since childhood I had been interested in the story or legend of El Q'anil, which had been passed by word of mouth from one generation to the next without a written text.[4] I thought, then, that the persistence of the legend of El Q'anil demonstrated the importance that this "history" had had for the Jakaltek people over the centuries. In other words, despite the changes and modernization of the indigenous areas of Guatemala such as Jacaltenango, the legend of El Q'anil still persisted as an ancestral relic that begged to be recovered and recorded for posterity in a written text.

As I have already mentioned, my interest in Jakaltek culture was born gradually as I became aware of the role that this tradition played within the concept of time and space in the Jakaltek history and worldview. My father once told me something that had happened to my grandfather, José Montejo, when he participated in the Mexican Revolution of 1910. (Many Guatemalans from the Guatemala-Mexico border region participated in this historical event.)

Before going off to fight in the revolution, my grandfather and his group went to seek the protection of El Q'anil, as was the custom at that time. My father says that after fighting the Villistas at the southern border, in the Hoja Blanca and Motozintla (Chiapas) region, my grandfather and other Jakalteks calmly sat down to clean their shotguns. Suddenly, one of the soldiers from the opposing army, who had hidden in the bushes, shot at my grandfather. The shot would have hit my grandfather in the head, but luckily the bullet struck the barrel of the gun that he was cleaning at that moment, saving his life. This is the type of miracle that was expected when the name of Q'anil was invoked before undertaking dangerous tasks, such as war. For this reason, the Q'anil cult was central to the indigenous cultures of the Cuchumatanes in ancient times. According to Juvenal Casaverde, "The alcaldes rezadores of the stock *niman coñob* must regularly visit K'anil's shrine, in relation with the traditional calendar, to perform rituals asking for his protection" (Casaverde 1976:33).

This tradition of visiting the sanctuary of Q'anil on the peak of the mountain that bears the same name is still practiced in modern times. When young men were "caught" for military service and forcibly taken to the general headquarters in distant cities (Quetzaltenango, Santa Cruz del Quiché, Zacapa, and Guatemala City), their parents would seek out the expert prayer makers and go to the sanctuary of Q'anil. There on the mountaintop they would burn candles and pray to God that Q'anil would protect their sons. They prayed that the guardian angel (Q'anil) would watch over their sons along their way, in front of them and behind them, so that they would return safe and sound to their community after serving in the military. It was said that, in ancient times, Q'anil gave signs and

warned the people of danger when it was necessary. Many declared that
when there was war, the *k'uh* (lightning bolt) would thunder on the mountain and a red flag would appear on the peak of Q'anil mountain as a sign
of danger and of the presence of the town's protector.[3]

This was how I began to become increasingly interested in the story of
Xhuwan Q'anil. Some elders, of blessed memory, including Antun Luk,
Kaxh Manel, Mat Tiyes, Kux Ahawis, and Manel Kaxh, lived near me in
Jacaltenango. People always gathered in their yards to listen to stories of
all kinds. It was in this type of gathering that I was immersed in the
mythical, poetic, and legendary world of my ancestors.

But things changed over the course of time, and during the 1970s
people seemed less concerned with oral tradition. Given these circum-
stances, I believed that the ancient cult to Q'anil would eventually become
a tale of superstition, void of historical importance to the people, but such
was not the case. In 1976–1977, an event of national transcendence made
me see that El Q'anil was not simply a myth from the past. Then-president
of Guatemala, General Kjell Eugenio Laugerud García, had announced to
the people that everyone should be prepared for the possibility of a war
with England over the matter of Belize. The people in the indigenous
communities were alarmed, as it was obvious that this would be a very
unequal war. In addition, the indigenous population of the Guatemalan
Highlands was fearful because, historically, they had always been used as
cannon fodder during wars. In other words, it seemed suicide for Guatemala, an underdeveloped country, to take on a military superpower like
Great Britain.

The army trucks soon arrived at the indigenous towns to "recruit" young
men for military service (in these communities the "military commis-
sioners" had the custom of forcibly seizing the young men to be taken to
the barracks). The elders again headed off to the summit of Mount Q'anil,
and there they burned candles to request protection for the young men
who had been captured for military service. I then realized that the name
and power of El Q'anil still maintained their vitality in the cultural tradition of the people, especially with regard to matters of war. Realizing this,
I became seriously interested in recording the story of El Q'anil, as I
listened to the different short and incomplete versions that the elders
began to relate. So it was that *El Q'anil*, the epic poem of the Jakaltek

people, began to take its written literary form. By writing *El Q'anil*, I believed I would be contributing to the rescue of the cultural legacy of my ancestors and maintaining the Maya creativity, which needed to be expressed. Now, *El Q'anil* has passed from oral tradition to written text and serves as a specific contribution of Maya culture to the great literary tradition of the indigenous peoples of the Americas.

This work is divided into two important sections. Preceding the first section, following ancient Maya tradition, is a "pórtico," which is the demonstration of respect that the grandparents demand on commencing an account of the names and heroic deeds of Maya ancestors. In other words, when communal knowledge (cultural stories and tradition) is involved, the *ahtz'ib'* (writer and storyteller) must begin his or her work with reverence and respect toward the memory of the ancestors who have given life to the people. The first half of the narration then describes the arrival of the Maya people in the territories they now occupy. The second half contains the body of the legend itself, which tells of the heroic feats of the Jakaltek heroes, with the central figure being Xhuwan Q'anil. The concept of cultural identity and an intimate relationship with one's birthplace grows out of this legend. Each and every Jakaltek child must return to his or her place of origin, where his or her umbilical cord has been buried. Near the end of the work, there is also mention of the participation of the "brother" from Chiapas, who arrives to help his brothers who are fighting against a strong and unknown enemy. This demonstrates that there was mutual collaboration during ancient times among the Maya peoples, who now find themselves divided by the international borders of the modern countries of Guatemala and Mexico.

As an ancient story *(payat tzoti')*, the legend of El Q'anil fulfills the characteristics of oral literature, which transcends time and space through the "telescopic" process of time (Bricker 1981; Gossen 1984). In this process, historical events and modern conflicts are interwoven in a dynamic cultural process that reflects ethnic conflicts. In this case, the legend of *El Q'anil* transports us to different times and historical events as it makes the remote current and vice versa. Thus, the legendary war at sea reminds us of Columbus's first vision (fourth voyage) of the storms and lightning that impeded the adventurers' arrival in Maya lands near the Yucatán peninsula:

El Q'anil: Man of Lightning

El Q'anil: Man of Lightning

Pórtico

Reverently, I wish to commence,
on the bank of the Blue River,[1]
the narration of the beginnings
and origin of my people,
which is also my own origin,
and the life of all our generations.
But first I must wash my face and hands
in the foam of the blue silence
that I may cross with grace and confidence
the mysterious pórtico
of my valiant ancestors, who live today
hidden like the water in the heart of the earth.[2]

Then, from the cliff, my sparkling eyes take
delight in the crystalline waters of the Blue River.
And then, on the peak of the Volcano of War,[3]
I burn incense, copal, and black tallow,
invoking with the clamor of a child
the presence of those lightning men[4]
who were once invincible warriors
on many bloody battlefields.

Or, is there anyone who does not know
the bravery and battle-hardened fury
of the heroic Jakaltek Maya?[5]

Even the vultures, perplexed, curse
that awful, bloody day long ago
when the greedy white invaders
stole the fertile lands and cornfields
of the great chief Jich Mam.

O, how small we are at home today
compared to the greatness of our ancestors,[6]
those heroes who were half-human, half-god,
who tirelessly blazed trails of light
in the heart of endless night
to bequeath to us a paradise of turtledoves,
who coo to us like virgins,
together with the clairvoyant *clarinero* birds,
the "dark spies of the seasons"
who order the clouds to rain.[7]

And if in the unforgettable past
the offerings of the *ninhq'omlom*
pleased the deities of Satkanh,[8]
I offer today my thoughts
poured out in abundant remembrances,
bringing to life the Jakaltek heroes
in this mythical epic of fire,
in the name of B'alunh Q'ana', our first father,
and Imox, our first mother,[9]
to whom I offer the bowl of *xahanb'al*[10]
that they may sip the exquisite essence
of the delicacies of beautiful Xajla'.[11]

one

The grandparents tell and our eyes confirm
that the mountains surrounding Xajla'
are intensely green like the jades
of B'alunh Q'ana', our first father.
Their splendid rivers flow beautiful and blue
like the necklaces of Imox, our first mother.
They are Jich Mam and Jich Mi', our origin.[12]
They gave us our fertile lands
and lovingly taught us to cultivate them,
sowing white corn and yellow corn.[13]

They poured their blood into our veins
and made us strong and courageous
like tigers, mountain lions, and jaguars.
They taught us the secrets of war,
to zealously defend our belongings,
our hills and our rivers,
our fields and our crops,
our trees, our animals,
our women, our daughters, our sons.[14]

They called us their chosen children
and taught us their sciences and their arts.
Then we made our hats and shirts;
our sandals came from the hide of the deer.[15]

And our women, with skillful hands,
wove blankets, skirts, belts, and blouses
and made with pride all our clothing,[16]
which they dyed with bright colors
using indigo and the blood of the annatto.[17]

We kneaded the mud and the clay
and formed our guardian angels;
we made our jugs, our pots,
our bowls, and our griddles.

Our wise ones also taught us
to keep the long count on the calendars
and to use the zero in our counts[18]
now hidden in hieroglyphs in the caves.

And our great coin, the cacao bean,
we ground and made into delicious drinks
served in gourds, long and shining
like our women's breasts.[19]

We also learned to read on the face of the sky
the days, months, and years of our existence,[20]
and thus the stars showed us
the good weather and the bad
because our guardian angels
accompanied us always, in our labors in the fields
and in bloody struggles against the enemy.

two

In the evenings when Father Sun sank[21]
dying behind the distant mountains,
our parents and grandparents would remind us
of the wise words of Jich Mam,
the "ancient father" and father of all our fathers:

"The past is the nourishment and honor of the present.
Let us walk in harmony upon this foundation
so that one day the history
still hidden from us may be ours.
May no one be left behind,
and may we all together . . . move forward!"[22]

In this way they told us of marvelous things
that tempered our warrior's hearts,
or at times moved us to tears,
when with sadness they told us:

The gods of nature became arrogant and
unleashed upon our great empire
rains of fire and flaming birds,
causing great jagged rocks to boil.
These enormous burning stones
ground to dust our clumsy, big-eared idols,
as our high priests and sorcerers,
like old toads or wounded moles,

hid with their pots, griddles, and incense burners
in dark caverns from which they never emerged alive.[23]

Kings and chiefs mourned the destruction
of our opulent city,
asking us to abandon temples and palaces
and seek a new and fruitful land
in which to settle permanently,
even against the will of some idols
who urinated, furious,
inside their boxes and gleaming bottle gourds.

Only thus did our heroic race disperse
in small, weak but valiant groups
that began to conquer virgin forests
and cross turbulent rivers.

Countless winters we wandered,
tangled in the forests' thickets,
until we reached the land of Ajul,[24]
where our kings decided to build.

Here we cut great blocks of *xaj* (limestone)
with which to build the city,
and therefore its name would be Xajla'.[25]

But our apathetic wise sorcerers,
who do, undo, and dismantle everything,
drew a doleful future with their scrawls,
certain that Ajul was not the appropriate place
and, besides, that the gods in the basket
had not signaled by sneezing.

Our leaders obeyed the *ahb'e* (soothsayers)
and continued on through mountains and forests,
guided by shrill monkeys and green parakeets,

which distracted our braggart chiefs and leaders
along the way with their antics.
We camped a long time in Meste',[26]
and from there, Jich Mam, our great father,
made his magic wand dance between his fingers
until it flew like a dove from his hands
and crossed the Blue River canyon,
disappearing from sight above the trees.[27]
The astonished royal retinue reached the place
where the flying wand had landed,
a plateau of fertile earth and great trees,
where birds and boars drank from these springs:
Ya' Smij, the vulture's spring,
Ya' Hol, spring of the deaf skull,
Sti' Ha' Pop, the water by the reeds.
Where the wand had penetrated the damp mud slabs,
a beautiful spring had begun to flow.
Its waters ran a short distance
before cascading down into the stream of the "Great River."
Therefore, those who had discovered the wonder cried,
"¡Ha' tx'otx', ha' tx'otx'! This is the place!"
Therefore, that spring was called Ha' Tx'otx'.

So it was that Jich Mam and his royal retinue,
through endless and exhausting days of labor,
raised the walls of our town,
imitating the colossal grandeur of Sat B'ak'ul
(source of the Blue River),
where the rain plunges into space
like the bitter tears of our ancestors.

But Jich Mam, faithful to God's plan,
decided to surround the settlement with k'uh,
which are man-gods, protectors,
who must be remembered always,
every hour, day, and season of the year.[28]

The k'uh were stationed in this way:
B'alunh Q'ana' himself would remain at Sat B'ak'ul,
the birthplace of the dawn.
Then he stationed Ochewal, Wiho, Wamu',
Sipoh, Q'anil Tx'otx', Yoq'ob' Hos, Kaj Icham,
Tzulb'al, Sat Tonhko', Swi' K'ej B'atz', Mapil Ch'en,
Yahb'al Kaq'e', Saj Tanhnaj Oy, Kaje,
Yinh Ch'en, Tx'ej Tunuk, Kulus Wakax,
Witenam, Nilq'o', Nhulnhulwi', K'ajb'al Txoh,
and Q'anil, the second of our fathers.
Thus closed the circle of guardians
who would forever protect the magnificent
and splendid Xajla', today Jacaltenango,
chosen city of the divine beings.

three

Our grandfathers continue telling that:
We had everything and lacked nothing.
Jich Mam and Jich Mi', our first parents,
taught us with ceaseless devotion.
From them we learned to play the marimba,
the slit drum, and the plaintive flute.
They also taught us to dance and sing
our joys and our sorrows
to the rhythm of the songs of the birds.

Extraordinary healers lived among us
who drove from our homes and our bodies
the illnesses and evil spirits that frequently pursued us.
Similarly, our terrible sorcerers,
wise and clairvoyant, forewarned us
of dangers and strange future events.[29]

Ah! Our dreams were peaceful
because our parents cared for us.

They were wise, great, and courageous,
and we declared our deep love and respect for them.
That is how we lived—without oppression,
without deceit or discrimination—
because all were equal and the same straw
covered the roofs of all our homes.[30]

But one day, we sensed something evil;
our pounding hearts told us so,
and our ears became hot and began to burn
like the ears of the pot over the fire.
Wech the fox[31] crossed our paths,
chilling us with his terrifying howls,
and the ominous owl[32] began also
to cackle at our bad luck
and mock our approaching destiny.

Only our parents calmed our spirits,
showing us with their large, glowing eyes
the path of the distant stars
over which we were to guide our steps,
steady, constant, and secure.

As valiant children of Xajla',
we were to achieve a great victory
and not fall to loathsome defeat.
Xajla', our bounteous birthplace,
was forever legendary and mysterious,
and again with great expectations
the victors emerged from here.[33]

four

One evening, as we were returning
from our fields and crops,
we stopped, astonished, along the way

as we heard the "tam, tam, tam, tam, tam!"
of the hoarse drums that drove
our women and children crazy
and made the nearby homes and mountains
resound loudly with their echo.[34]
"What is it?" we wondered, bewildered,
and soon we reached our homes,
where we heard the important news.

"All the young men of the region
must present themselves in the plaza before Jich Mam,
and from them will be chosen the strongest,
the bravest, and the most valiant
to lead a battalion
to a distant war in a faraway place,
beyond our own mountains
and far beyond the sea itself."[35]

In the plaza, women, children, and elderly
also gathered with a great hubbub
to witness the selection of the warriors.
Then Jich Mam stepped forward in great majesty,
and raising his voice, he spoke gravely
to the crowd that listened in silence.

"Sons of Xajla', ever courageous,
with a heavy heart I bring you word
that, across the sea, a friendly city
is being destroyed by its enemies
who fight from the sea
and use strange and powerful weapons
with which they can kill many people
and raze entire cities.[36]
And as the great renown of our people
is already known even in the most remote places,
we are now invited, and with great honor,

to share our strength with them
and to offer them our aid as friends.
Courage then, my heroic warriors,
as a bloody battle awaits us
from which we must emerge victorious."[37]

Thus spoke Jich Mam among the people
as with his golden staff he touched
those most adept for battle
and especially the most courageous.

five

The first complaints were heard from onlookers
who insulted the chosen men.
Then the sorcerers of night stepped forth,
and with them the experts in the most occult,
shouting and challenging the favorites.[38]

"Let the chosen ones stay here with their women
and continue working their fields in peace.
How can they challenge and defeat
the enemy who fights under the water?
How can they stop his poison arrows
if this is a war of occult powers?[39]
We, on the other hand, can do anything."
So they spoke, demonstrating their powers:[40]

"I can turn myself into a serpent," said one.
"I can become a fierce wild cat," said another.
And the rest declared: "I can turn into a jaguar."
"I become a dangerous toad."
"I become a poisonous horsefly."
"I become a shrewd fox."
"I become a rabid dog."

So they proclaimed, and their metamorphoses began.
Some writhed, others jumped or growled,
and others roared threateningly,
causing panic among the people.
Ah, in those days Xajla' had everything
because even Matzwalil, the devil himself,[41]
played among us with his madness,
upsetting everything with his evil deeds.

Jich Mam observed the malevolent sorcerers
and doubted whether those foolish ones
could even return to Xajla' alive.[42]
In spite of his doubts, he began to prepare them
with strange rituals of fire and blood.
It was not a large number that were prepared;
only twenty-eight were chosen,
all of them sorcerers and skilled experts
in the forbidden and the supernatural.[43]

"We don't need anyone else," they shouted
as they strutted proudly among the people.
"Let no one dare compare himself to us,
because we are the only ones in this town
who can cause suffering to those who disparage us.
All we need now are porters
who will carry our sleeping mats, our cooking pots,
our drinking gourds, and our food,
because we, the 'chosen ones,'
shall carry only our powers."[44]

Thus spoke our conceited sorcerers,
as if they had already defeated the enemy.
Meanwhile, with extreme arrogance,
they marched back and forth, packing their bags
and then demanding volunteers
to accompany them as bearers.[45]

"I'll go!" volunteered Xhuwan Q'anil.
He was quite small to be a bearer,
but was proud to offer his services
carrying his own belongings and those of the sorcerers.

"I'll go too!" yelled another.
"And me and me . . ." volunteered others,
but this time only two were chosen.
And so was formed the Xajla' battalion,
of several sorcerers and two young bearers
who, not even knowing where they were going,
were ready and willing to fight the enemy.

six

That night Xhuwan did not sleep, thinking
how to avert the certain death
toward which the conceited sorcerers were heading.
He wondered how they could return alive from the adventure
and some day be reunited with their wives
and children and continue working their fields
and by grace continue to take delight
in their blue rivers and distant horizons.[46]

The answer lay in the cliffs of Sat B'ak'ul,[47]
where B'alunh Q'ana', the first of the lightning men,
has kept watch over Xajla' through the centuries,
hurling his blazing lightning bolts through the clouds
or making the mountains tremble and the forests shudder
when danger lies in wait for us along our way.

During the night, Xhuwan went off alone,
seeking the face of Sat B'ak'ul,
there where the torrential rains are born,
beyond the first songs of the Blue River.[48]

Xhuwan appeared before the k'uh, requesting
those powers that make the clouds roar
and hurl powerful bolts of lightning toward the earth.
"Xhuwan," responded B'alunh Q'ana', "my powers are so great
that you could not contain them in your hands;
you could easily destroy the world.[49]
There to the west of Xajla' stands Kaje.
Go see him, because Kaje is less powerful than I."

So Xhuwan left the crags of Sat B'ak'ul,
the birthplace of the dawns,
and hastened to the tremendous Kaje,
who ceaselessly cares for our town
from the place where the sun hides at night.

Xhuwan begged the great k'uh to share his powers.
"No, Xhuwan," responded the k'uh.
"This dark purple shirt that I wear[50]
contains the full force of my power,
and you could never control it.
Go to my younger brothers,
for they will surely help you."

Xhuwan left in search of the k'uh
who watch over the town from the north.
These were Saj Tanhnaj Oy,[51] Tzulb'al,
and Yoq'ob' Hos,
whose strange name means "egg goiter."
Yoq'ob' Hos made fun of Xhuwan, saying,
"Here, I give you my powers,"
and set before Xhuwan a plate with two eggs.[52]

Desperate, Xhuwan ran like a deer
toward the magnificence of Q'anil,
the father k'uh located south of the city.

Xhuwan stood under the shadow of the k'uh saying,
"Father Q'anil, give me your powers."
Q'anil answered, surprised,
"Tell me, Xhuwan, why do you ask for my powers?"

"Tomorrow my brothers will go to fight a war
in aid of an oppressed people far from here.
As the fame of the warriors of Xajla'
has reached their ears, they now ask us
to fight the enemy that uses strange weapons
and fights from the sea, under the waves.
But our battalion is made up of sorcerers.
They are not warriors! What can they do?
We bearers will perish with them in that sea,
because all they can do is turn themselves
into ferocious beasts or strange creatures
that will be targets for the enemy on the beach.

"Therefore, Father Q'anil," Xhuwan declared,
"I want to offer my life for those people.
It matters not that my blood be spilled
and that I never return to this land,
as long as they achieve peace and are saved.[53]
Thus I wish to perpetuate the name of my people.
Give me, therefore, the powers I need and long for
so I may depart tomorrow with the morning star."

Hearing this touching tale,
the great k'uh responded, saying,
"Are you willing to leave behind all that you have
and never return to your town
or change your mind once you have the powers?"
"I have already made that decision," Xhuwan said.
"Then lie down and receive my powers."

Xhuwan lay down, and at that moment there was

a great thunderclap, and many lightning bolts
lit up the darkened sky.
The voice of Q'anil was heard through the lightning,
"Arise and put on this yellow shirt[54]
that holds all the powers you asked for."
As Q'anil spoke,
Xhuwan stood up and rubbed his hands with satisfaction.

seven

When Xhuwan rushed back to the village,
many lights from crackling pine torches
already glowed in wakening houses.
Nearly in tears, he bid farewell to his parents,
brothers, sisters, and relatives.
Only he knew that the trip was final
and that he would never see them again.

The sorcerers arrived at the plaza yawning
and throwing their bags to the ground.
Then they shouted boastfully:
"Where are those bearers of ours?
Quick, now, porters! Clean up this mess!"[55]

The expedition set off in darkness
under the final blessing of Jich Mam.
Elders, women, and children wept
as our valiant warriors
gallantly commenced their journey.

The mountains closed around the travelers,
who were illuminated by the lightning bugs that blinked
on and off playfully on the dark path ahead
like tiny stars beneath their feet.
From time to time the porters stopped
to remove their tumplines when they felt

their heads aching or their backs cramping,
while the sorcerers talked loudly,
looking scornfully at the bearers
and believing themselves to be the best.

Xhuwan, with the heavy load on his back,
kept his secrets to himself and his powers hidden.[56]
Who would have imagined that there walked a k'uh
with all his powers and lightning bolts of destruction?

Danger awaited them at every turn.
Hungry wolves attacked the exhausted bearers,
who lagged behind,
and those who led the way were ambushed
by brambles and poisonous snakes.
But on they went, resolute, beneath the burning sun
and beneath torrential rains that sapped their strength.
Their path through canyons and mountains was laid out for
them, and they did not stop although death itself tormented them,
casting stones and fruits at them from the trees,
as if imitating the screeching monkeys.

eight

Deep in the Cuchumatán Mountains, at Tenb'al May,[57]
the sorcerers gave the order to rest and make camp.
Their wide-necked drinking gourds were empty,
and without water they could not mix their tasty drinks
of corn dough and cocoa in their bowls.

"Porters," shouted the boastful sorcerers,
"we're hungry and thirsty.
You will go to bring us water
from the spring over there among the pines.
Quick now!" they said, spitting on the ground.

"The water is close by; I'll go alone," said Xhuwan.
"I'll go with you," his companion said.
(This is the one we call Juan Méndez.)[58]

As they walked toward the spring,
Xhuwan's companion blurted out,
"If only we could stop those conceited sorcerers
from marching blindly toward sure death."
"We can," Xhuwan answered immediately.
"Would you be willing to leave your parents,
your brothers and sisters, all that you have
if your wishes could be fulfilled?"

"Yes, I am willing," answered his friend.
"Good," said Xhuwan. "Then I will have a companion.
Lie on your back on the ground,
and I will jump over you three times."[59]

Three times Xhuwan jumped, passing over his friend,
and when the strange ceremony ended,
the bearer stood up and Xhuwan pointed,
"Look at that huge pine tree; I will fell it."
Saying this, Xhuwan tensed his muscles
and leapt, lighting up the area
with a lightning bolt that blinded his friend.
Astonished, Juan Méndez covered his ears,
anticipating the crack of thunder that followed.
Then a great bolt of lightning sliced the tree
in two, from its crown to its roots.
An uncontrolled blaze soon burned
in the pitch of its old heart.

When the bearer opened his eyes,
Xhuwan was standing in front of him, watching
the fire as if nothing had happened.

"This is our power. Now try yours,"
said Xhuwan to his stunned companion.
Without a word, his friend tensed his muscles
and gave the leap that produced lightning,
then thunder, and a terrifying bolt
took aim at another enormous pine.
But the trial went wrong, and Juan Méndez
was trapped in the crack of the trunk.[60]
Seeing this, Xhuwan transformed himself again,
and another powerful bolt streaked through the sky,
causing the great tree to explode into splinters.

"Let's try again," said Xhuwan.
This time, the apprentice appeared as a raging tempest
and shattered several trees.
"Well done!" cried Xhuwan excitedly.
"Now I will plant trees to replace those we have destroyed."[61]
Saying this, like a serpent of fire,
he cut off the tops of the fallen trees
and then planted them anew in the forest.

As they practiced, a light drizzle
began to fall from the cloudless blue sky.[62]
Hurriedly, they filled the large drinking gourds
and quietly returned to the camp.
On the way, Xhuwan warned his friend
not to say anything to the malicious sorcerers,
who might become very angry
and cause trouble for them along the way.

nine

When Xhuwan and his companion returned,
the agitated sorcerers' owl eyes were wide with surprise,
as they argued about the sudden occurrence:

"Did you hear that?" said one. "No one can
cause lightning and thunder like I can.
I can make rain fall from a cloudless sky."
"Lies," said another. "You didn't do that;
I am the only one with those great powers."

Xhuwan said nothing, but his heart was laughing
as he watched them claiming powers they lacked.[63]

Then the sorcerers scolded the bearers,
"What took you so long?
Was the water far away up the hill?"

But there were two diviners (ahb'e) among them,
who soon realized that the two bearers were the ones
who had caused those strange natural phenomena.[64]

So it was that one of them suddenly said,
"From now on you two
will no longer carry packs on your backs."
"Each of us will carry our own things," said the other.
Hearing this, the others fell silent.
They could not believe the humble porters
possessed the power that explodes in the sky.

They looked at each other
and recognized that not one of them
had those powers of fire in his hands.
Thus, each one picked up his own pack,
and they marched on through mountains,
valleys, and swamps for many days
until finally they reached the sea.[65]

Our elders do not tell us how they crossed,
but they continue narrating the battle scene like this:

There were many dead men spread
like shells all along the beach,
and broken bows and dropped shields
were scattered everywhere.
Seeing this, the old sorcerers paled
and retreated, their hearts filled with fear,
wanting to return home.

The sorcerers said with great consternation,
"We can fight as men
and even turn ourselves into beasts,
but either way, as men or beasts,
they will easily defeat and kill us."[66]
Xhuwan and his friend said they would not turn back.
They would never flee, not even from death itself.
"Jich Mam has sent us," Xhuwan said, "and if we run from here,
we will bring dishonor on Xajla'."[67]
A short time later, their packs on their backs,
our warriors presented themselves
before the king, whose face fell when he saw them.

"What kind of joke is this?" exclaimed the king.[68]
"Those dead men on the beach, being eaten by vultures,
were an army of good warriors.
How is it that some barefoot porters
come before me today, unarmed and speaking
a language no one here has ever heard?[69]
Or perhaps you have come to insult me?"
The men from Xajla' paid no heed to the king's comments.
Instead, reading his face, they answered without hesitation,
"We have come to fight."

The king waved them away, laughing bitterly.
"You poor things had better return to your home,
because you will not even be able to set foot on the beach."

ten

Our warriors declared, impassioned,
"Since leaving Xajla' many days ago
we have suffered all along the way;
and if we have crossed mountains, valleys, and seas,
it is because we have accepted the invitation
to offer our lives in this war.
We have not come to mourn the dead
and return home as simple travelers.
Show us the enemy and let us fight."

"What? Let you fight just to die?
The few of you against such an army?
You must be crazy!" replied the king.

The king sent four warriors to the beach
to locate the enemy under the waves.[70]
They soon returned, gravely wounded,
their faces and bodies bleeding.
"Now you see; we are lost!" shouted the king.
"And if you crazy men wish to die,
go ahead and sacrifice yourselves, but we here
have enough dead to bury already."

At that, Xhuwan rose and spoke to the sorcerers.
"Brothers, what can snakes, cats,
monkeys, jaguars, and toads
do in this war we must fight?
Oh no! Then everyone will know that our people
sent only fools and not fighters.
Retreat with the king to a safe place
and let the two of us begin,
because we are now the only hope."
The two porters marched toward the sea smiling.

They were about to begin the battle
when a smiling man greeted them, saying,
"I am your brother from Chiapas.[71] In dreams
I learned of your mission, and I am here to help.
Allow me to act first."

Then the sky blazed with lightning, thunder exploded,
and a crackling lightning bolt struck the sea,
throwing back its waves and revealing the enemy.[72]
Xhuwan and his companion followed with fury.
Again and again they unleashed their lightning bolts,
pounding the bloodied waves of the sea.[73]

Suddenly the king appeared on the shore,
shouting over the noise of battle,
"Stop! Leave some seed of them.
They are owners of a great culture
and makers of beautiful silks."[74]

Xhuwan answered, "Have we come from so far away
to fail to eradicate these demons?
Well, as you wish; you are the king,
but when war breaks out on the day of Oxlanh B'en,[75]
we shall indeed return,
and no one will act in our place.
Then we will obliterate this enemy."

The king, satisfied, called down from the dunes
to the few enemies who were still alive.
They came out of the water holding up white flags pleading,
"Have mercy on us; our men have abandoned their fury,
and we come to your shores in defeat."

The king jumped for joy and said,
"Once Xajla' nourished our dreams,
and behold, this handful of warriors

confirms it all in the face of our disbelief.
It was an error to think that these men
came simply as fools, to die.
Now their courage brings us to reality,
changing our defeat into victory.
We shall feast then for three days
and give them the highest honors of the court
and the gifts and tributes they deserve."[76]

To this, our warriors responded,
"Do not worry about us at all;
we have accomplished our mission
and now we prefer to return quickly
to the distant place of our origin."

Thus the warriors declined the tribute,
choosing the peace of humility
over the world's honors and pleasures.

eleven

Our elders still speak in awe
of that moving return of the victors,
but they also keep as a heavy secret
the name of the place they had gone
and the way they crossed the great sea.[77]

The elders go on, telling that:
When the warriors were approaching Xajla',
Xhuwan and his companion told the others,
"You can return to Xajla' without us.
We who carried out that great slaughter
are no longer like the rest of our people,
and we have already sworn never to return to Xajla'
and never to see our own families again.[78]

"Just tell them that we are alive
and that our powers prevent us from returning.
We shall hide ourselves and our golden arrows
south of the town, on the mountain of Q'anil,
the home of the father who gave us the powers,
and from there we will protect Xajla' from danger,
raising our banners in the clouds
and the thunder of our voice on the wind.[79]
Thus we shall be with you always."

The sorcerers ended the long journey
crying and sniffling sadly,
like children who have lost their parents
or dogs who have lost their masters.
The news of their return brought joy to Xajla', and
the townspeople followed the paths out to meet them,
surrounding them immediately with great rejoicing,
because no one had died in strange lands.[80]

They soon noticed there were only twenty-eight men.
Everyone began to count on their fingers and toes,
and two were missing. The two porters!
"Where are they? Or perhaps they have been killed?"

Then the owl-eyed sorcerers,
catching their breath, responded in this way:
"We are victorious; the victory is ours
thanks to the porters and to the brother from Chiapas
(the man of lightning we call Juan Carmelo).[81]
They could not return with us,
but from now on they shall live on Mount Q'anil,
very close to the town. They are now k'uh,
men of lightning, guardians of Xajla' and Chiapas,
of whom we should be proud.
They are no longer like us, they are now different,
but even so, we are still theirs.

From the peak of Mount Q'anil they will watch over us
and protect us with their blazing lightning bolts.
So they have promised and so it will be."[82]

The families of the heroes were proud
and received honors as privileged sons and daughters.
Gradually this alleviated their grief.
Jich Mam held celebrations in the plaza,
while a commission of Maya priests
climbed El Q'anil, the Volcano of War,
to sacrifice turkeys and burn candles and copal
in honor of these new heroes of Xajla'.

Up there on the peak of El Q'anil,
though we do not see them, we feel their breathing,
we feel them living and speaking;
and when there is danger in storms,
or poisonous snakes lie in wait for us
in the thick trunks of the trees,
then they hurl their lightning bolts,
driving away the evil that seeks our lives.

Our elders believed and related all of this
with painful memories of the past,
and thus they have passed it on to their children,
to their children's children, through all generations,
until it reached us, their descendants
who live today in Xajla', Jacaltenango.[83]

El Q'anil: El hombre rayo

El Q'anil: El hombre rayo

Reverente, quiero comenzar
junto al Río Azul,
a narrar los principios
y el origen de mi gente,
que es también mi propio origen,
y la vida de nuestras generaciones.
Pero antes he de lavarme la cara y las manos
en la espuma del azul silencio
para luego, con paso firme, penetrar airoso
a través del pórtico misterioso
de mis bravos ancestros, quienes viven hoy
opacos como el agua en el corazón de la tierra.

Luego, desde la barranca recrear mis ojos
vivarachos en las cristalinas aguas del Río Azul
o tal vez quemar pom, copal y cera negra
en la cúspide del volcán de la guerra,
invocando con clamores de niño
la presencia de aquellos hombres rayos
que un día fueron héroes invencibles
en los sangrientos campos de batalla.

¿Habrá quien que no conozca
del arrojo y de la aguerrida furia
del indómito maya jakalteko?

Aun los zopilotes maldicen confusos
aquel cruento día lejano y fatal
en que los invasores blancos y ambiciosos
despojaron al gran cacique Jich Mam
de sus fértiles tierras y maizales.

Oh, qué pequeños somos hoy en casa
ante la grandeza de nuestros abuelos;
aquellos héroes mitad hombres, mitad dioses
que incansables abrieron brechas luminosas
en el corazón de la noche perpetua
para legarnos un paraíso de tórtolas
que han de arrullarnos como vírgenes,
junto con los clarividentes clarineros,
"negros espías del tiempo"
que ordenan a las nubes que llueva.

Y si en el pretérito imborrable
las ofrendas de los *ninhq'omlom* (rezadores)
fueron del agrado de las deidades de Satkanh,
yo ofrendo hoy mis pensamientos
vertidos en pletóricas remembranzas,
haciendo resucitar a los héroes jakaltekos
en esta mítica epopeya de fuego,
en el nombre de B'alunh Q'ana', nuestro primer padre,
y en el de Imox, nuestra primera madre,
a quienes ofrendo el tazón del *xahanb'al*
para que sorban la esencia exquisita
de los manjares de la bella Xajla'.

uno

Los abuelos dicen y nuestros ojos lo confirman
que las montañas que rodean a Xajla'
son intensamente verdes como los jades
de B'alunh Q'ana', nuestro primer padre.
Sus espléndidos ríos corren azulosos y bellos
como los collares de Imox, la primera madre.
Jich Mam y Jich Mi' son ellos, nuestro origen.
Ellos nos dieron nuestras fértiles tierras
y nos enseñaron con amor a cultivarlas
de maíz blanco y de maíz amarillo.

También vertieron su sangre en nuestras venas
y nos hicieron fuertes y valerosos
como tigres, pumas y jaguares,
enseñándonos además los trucos de la guerra
para cuidar con celo nuestras pertenencias,
nuestros cerros, nuestros ríos,
nuestros campos y milperíos;
nuestros árboles, nuestros animales,
nuestras mujeres, nuestras hijas y nuestros hijos.

Ellos nos llamaron sus hijos predilectos
y nos enseñaron sus ciencias y sus artes.
Entonces hacíamos nuestros sombreros y *kapixhayes;*
nuestros caites hacíamos con piel de venado.

Y nuestras mujeres, con prodigiosas manos,
tejían mantas, cortes, cintas y huipiles
y hacían con orgullo toda nuestra ropa,
la cual teñían luego con vivos colores
utilizando el jiquilete y la sangre del achiote.

Amasábamos con destreza el lodo y el barro
y hacíamos imágenes de ángeles protectores;
hacíamos nuestras tinajas, nuestras ollas,
nuestras escudillas y nuestros comales.

Nuestros sabios nos enseñaron así mismo
a llevar cuentas largas en los calendarios
y a utilizar el cero en nuestros conteos
escondidos hoy en jeroglíficos en las cavernas.

Y nuestra gran moneda, el cacao,
molido lo tomábamos en posoles sabrosos
servidos en largas y brillantes jícaras
como las tetas de nuestras mujeres.

Aprendimos también a leer en la faz del cielo
los días, meses y años de nuestra existencia,
y así los luceros nos señalaban
el tiempo bueno y el tiempo malo
puesto que nuestros ángeles protectores
nos acompañaban siempre en las faenas del campo
y en las luchas sangrientas contra el enemigo.

dos

Por las tardes cuando el Padre Sol, moribundo,
declinaba detrás de las lejanas montañas,
nuestros padres y abuelos solían recordarnos
las sabias palabras de Jich Mam,
el "anciano padre" y padre de nuestros padres:

"El pasado es alimento y honra del presente.
Sobre esta base caminemos en concordia
para que un día sea también nuestra la historia
que aún se esconde ante nuestros ojos.
Que nadie se quede detrás de los demás
y que todos juntos . . . ¡avancemos!"

Así nos contaban cosas maravillosas,
templando nuestros corazones de guerreros,
o haciéndonos llorar a veces
cuando con tristeza nos relataban:

Cuando los dioses naturales se ensoberbecieron,
precipitaron lluvias de fuego y pájaros ardientes
sobre nuestro gran imperio,
haciendo hervir grandes piedras picudas
que cual enormes y candentes tenamastes
aplastaron a nuestros torpes ídolos orejudos,
mientras nuestros brujos o *nawales*,
como viejos sapos o topos heridos,

se escondieron en cóncavas y negras cavernas
juntamente con sus ollas, comales y sahumerios,
y de donde jamás salieron con vida.

Reyes y caciques lloraron la destrucción
de nuestra ciudad opulenta,
pidiéndonos abandonar templos y palacios
para buscar nuevas y pródigas tierras
dónde establecernos definitivamente,
aun en contra de la voluntad de algunos ídolos
quienes se orinaban coléricos
dentro de los cacaxtes y pumpos relucientes.

Solamente así se dispersó nuestra raza indómita
en pequeños grupos débiles pero aguerridos
que fueron conquistando montañas vírgenes
y cruzando ríos de corrientes turbulentas.

Incontables inviernos peregrinamos,
enredados en las marañas de los bosques,
hasta que llegamos a la tierra de Ajul,
donde nuestros líderes dispusieron acampar.

Aquí tallamos grandes bloques de *xaj* (sarro)
con los que quisimos construir el pueblo
y que por eso su nombre sería Xajla'.

Más, nuestros sabios brujos abúlicos,
que todo lo atan, desatan y desbaratan,
señalaron el futuro con sus funestos garabatos,
asegurando que Ajul no era el lugar propicio
y además que los ídolos del cacaxte
no habían dado su señal estornudando.

Nuestros principales obedecieron a los adivinos
y siguieron avanzando por montes y bosques,

guiados por micos chillones y verdes pericos
que en el trayecto distraían con sus juegos
a nuestros jefes y líderes.
En Meste' se acampó largo tiempo,
y desde allí, Jich Mam, nuestro gran padre,
bailoteó entre sus dedos la varita mágica
la cual voló de sus manos como paloma
que cruzó zumbando la barranca del Río Azul
hasta perderse de vista sobre los bosques.
La comitiva real llegó asombrada
donde la vara zumbadora se había clavado.
Era ésta una meseta fértil de frondosos árboles,
donde aves y jabalíes bebían de las fuentes de
Ya' Smij, la fuente del zopilote;
Ya' Hol, la fuente de la calavera sorda;
Sti' Ha' Pop, a orillas del agua de esteras.
Donde la vara se clavó entre húmedas lajas,
había brotado un hermoso manantial
cuyas aguas corrían regando un corto trecho
hasta precipitarse en la cañada del "Gran Río".
Por eso, los que hallaron el prodigio gritaron,
"¡Ha' tx'otx', ha' tx'otx'! ¡Ésta es la tierra!"
Y por eso, Ha' Tx'otx' se llamó esta fuente.

Así fue como Jich Mam y su real comitiva,
en interminables y fatigosas jornadas,
alzaron los muros de nuestro pueblo,
simulando la imponencia titánica de Sat B'ak'ul
(lugar donde nace el Río Azul),
en donde se precipita la lluvia al vacío
como el llanto amargo de nuestros ancestros.

Pero Jich Mam, por designio de Dios,
dispuso rodear al poblado con k'uh (rayos),
que son hombres-dioses, protectores,

a quienes había que recordar siempre
en cada hora, día y época del año.

A los k'uh se les ubicó de esta forma:
El mismo B'alunh Q'ana' se quedaría en Sat B'ak'ul,
el lugar donde nacen las auroras.
Luego se ubicó a Ochewal, Wiho, Wamu',
Sipoh, Q'anil Tx'otx', Yoq'ob' Hos, Kaj Icham,
Tzulb'al, Sat Tonhko', Swi' K'ej B'atz', Mapil Ch'en,
Yahb'al Kaq'e', Saj Tanhnaj Oy, Kaje,
Yinh Ch'en, Tx'ej Tunuk, Kulus Wakax,
Witenam, Nilq'o', Nhulnhulwi', K'ajb'al Txoh
y Q'anil, nuestro segundo padre.
Cerrando así el círculo de cuidadores
que protegerían para siempre a la elegante
y pomposa Xajla', hoy Jacaltenango,
pueblo escogido de las divinidades.

tres

Nuestros abuelos continúan contando que:
Nosotros todo lo teníamos y nada nos faltaba,
Jich Mam y Jich Mi', nuestros primeros padres,
nos enseñaron con incansable empeño.
Por ellos aprendimos a tocar la marimba,
el tun y la quejosa chirimía.
Y también, nos enseñaron a danzar y a cantar vivamente
nuestras alegrías y nuestros dolores
al compás de los trinos de los pájaros.

Extraordinarios curanderos habían con nosotros
que de nuestras casas y de nuestros cuerpos
apartaban enfermedades y malos espíritus
que con frecuencia solían perseguirnos.
Del mismo modo, nuestros sabios y videntes

nos anunciaban con tiempo los peligros
y extraños acontecimientos venideros.

¡Ah! Nuestros sueños eran tranquilos
porque nuestros padres cuidaban de nosotros.
Ellos eran sabios, grandes y valientes,
y les profesábamos mucho cariño y respeto.
Es así como vivíamos—sin opresiones,
sin engaños ni discriminaciones—
pues todos éramos iguales y era la misma paja
que cubría el techo de nuestras casas.

Pero un día, algo malo presentimos;
nuestros corazones con sus brincos nos lo decían
y nuestras orejas se calentaban y ardían
como las orejas de las ollas sobre el fuego.
En nuestros caminos se cruzaba el *wech* (gato de monte)
estremeciéndonos con sus horribles chillidos,
y el tecolote agorero comenzaba también
a carcajearse de nuestra adversa suerte,
y se burlaba del rodar de nuestro destino.

Sólo nuestros padres calmaban nuestros ánimos,
señalándonos con sus grandes ojos en llama
el camino de los astros lejanos
por donde teníamos que conducir nuestros pasos
firmes, constantes y seguros.

Como aguerridos hijos de Xajla' que éramos,
debíamos lograr una gran victoria
y no caer en la detestable derrota.
Xajla', nuestra cuna florecida,
era por siempre legendaria y misteriosa,
y otra vez con gran expectación
de aquí volvieron a surgir los vencedores.

cuatro

Una tarde, mientras retornábamos
de nuestros campos y milperíos,
nos detuvimos en el camino asombrados
al escuchar el "¡tam, tam, tam, tam, tam!"
de los roncos tambores que enloquecían
a nuestras mujeres y a nuestros hijos
y que hacían retumbar con estrépito
las casas y los montes cercanos.
"¿Qué es eso?" nos preguntábamos confusos
y así lentamente llegamos a nuestras casas
donde supimos la gran noticia.

"Todos los hombres más jóvenes de la comarca
debían presentarse en la plaza ante Jich Mam,
y ahí serían escogidos los más fuertes,
los más bravos y los más valientes
que irían al frente de un batallón
a una guerra allá lejos, muy lejos,
más allá de nuestras propias montañas
y mucho más allá del mismo mar".

En la plaza, mujeres, niños y viejos
también acudieron con mucho bullicio
a presenciar la selección de los guerreros.
Entonces Jich Mam se adelantó majestuoso
y, levantando la voz, habló con grave acento
al gentío que lo escuchaba silencioso.

"Hijos de Xajla', por siempre valerosos,
con pesar en el corazón les comunico
que, al otro lado del mar, un pueblo amigo
está siendo destruido por sus enemigos
que luchan metidos en las aguas del mar
y que usan armas desconocidas y poderosas

con las que pueden matar a mucha gente
y arrasar con pueblos completos.
Y como la buena fama de nuestro pueblo
se conoce ya en los más remotos lugares,
estamos ahora invitados, y con mucha honra,
a compartir con ellos lo que valemos
y a prestarles como amigos nuestro auxilio.
Fortaleza pues, mis heróicos guerreros,
que una sangrienta lucha nos espera
y de la cual debemos salir vencedores".

Así habló Jich Mam entre la gente
mientras con su vara dorada tocaba
a los más dispuestos a la lucha
y en especial a los más llenos de bravura.

cinco

Los primeros disgustos brotaron de los curiosos
quienes dirigían insultos a los escogidos.
Entonces se presentaron los brujos nocturnos
y con ellos los conocedores de lo más oculto
gritando y desafiando a los preferidos.

"Que los escogidos se queden con sus mujeres
y que sigan labrando sus campos tranquilos.
¿Cómo podrán ellos combatir y vencer
al enemigo que lucha bajo las aguas?
¿Cómo podrán ellos parar sus dardos venenosos
si ésta es una guerra de poderes ocultos?
En cambio, nosotros todo lo podremos hacer".
Así decían ellos, exhibiendo sus poderes:

"Yo sé convertirme en culebra", dijo uno.
"Yo en colérico gato", dijo otro.

Y los demás decían: "Yo en jaguar".
"Yo en peligroso sapo".
"Yo en tábano venenoso".
"Yo en astuto zorro".
"Yo en perro rabioso".

Así pregonaban todos, metamorfoseándose.
Unos se retorcían, otros saltaban o gruñían,
y los otros rugían amenazantes,
infundiendo pánico entre la gente.
Ah, en aquel tiempo Xajla' tenía de todo
porque hasta el mismo Matzwalil, el diablo,
jugueteaba entre nosotros con sus locuras,
provocándonos disturbios con sus maldades.

Jich Mam observaba a los malévolos brujos
y dudaba si aquellos insensatos
podrían retornar aún con vida a Xajla'.
A pesar de sus dudas, siguió preparándolos
con extraños ritos de fuego y de sangre.
No era gran número el que se alistaba;
veintiocho eran solamente los escogidos,
y todos ellos brujos y hábiles conocedores
de lo vedado y sobrenatural.

"Con nosotros es suficiente", gritaban,
paseándose orgullosos entre la gente.
"Que nadie más se compare con nosotros,
porque nosotros somos los únicos del pueblo
que podemos hacer padecer al que nos humille.
Ahora sólo necesitamos a los cargadores
que llevarán nuestros petates, nuestras ollas,
nuestros tecomates y nuestros posoles,
porque nosotros los 'escogidos'
cargaremos sólo con nuestros poderes".

Así hablan nuestros brujos vanidosos
como si de veras ya fueran vencedores.
Mientras tanto, con exagerada arrogancia
iban y venían preparando sus maletas
y exigiendo luego hombres voluntarios
que los acompañasen en misión de maleteros.

"¡Yo iré de maletero!" se ofreció Xhuwan Q'anil.
Era bastante pequeño como para ser maletero,
pero era su orgullo ofrecer sus servicios
cargando con lo suyo y con lo de los brujos.

"¡Yo también voy!" gritó otro.
"Y yo, y yo . . .", gritaron otros ofreciéndose,
pero esa vez sólo dos fueron los escogidos.
Así quedó pues preparado el batallón de Xajla'
con varios brujos y dos jóvenes maleteros
quienes, sin imaginar siquiera adónde iban,
muy dispuestos querían combatir al enemigo.

seis

Por la noche Xhuwan no durmió, pensando
cómo evitar la muerte segura
a que caminaban los brujos vanidosos.
Pensaba cómo retornar vivos de la aventura
y volver a ver algún día a sus mujeres,
a sus hijos y seguir cultivando sus campos,
y con gracia, seguir recreando sus ojos
en sus azules ríos y horizontes lejanos.

La respuesta estaría en los riscos de Sat B'ak'ul,
donde B'alunh Q'ana', el primer hombre rayo,
mantiene vigilancia sobre Xajla' por los siglos,
arrojando quemantes rayos entre las nubes

o sacudiendo montañas y estremeciendo bosques
cuando algún peligro nos acecha en el sendero.

Durante la noche, Xhuwan se alejó solitario,
buscando la muralla de Sat B'ak'ul,
allí donde nacen las lluvias torrenciales,
más allá de los primeros cantos del Río Azul.

Xhuwan se presentó ante el k'uh, pidiendo
esos poderes que hacen rugir a las nubes
y lanzar estruendosos rayos a la tierra.
A su petición, B'alunh Q'ana' le respondió,
"Xhuwan, mis poderes son tan grandes
que no podrías contenerlos en tus manos,
destruyendo entonces fácilmente el mundo.
Allá al occidente de Xajla' está Kaje.
Camina a verlo, que Kaje es menor que yo".

Así abandonó Xhuwan los peñascos de Sat B'ak'ul,
el lugar donde nacen las auroras,
y se dirigió presuroso al tremendo Kaje,
que por el lado donde el sol se oculta
cuida a nuestro pueblo sin demora.

Xhuwan pidió compartir con el k'uh sus poderes.
"No, Xhuwan", le respondió el k'uh.
"Esta camisa púrpura que yo visto
contiene toda la fuerza de mi poder,
y tú no podrías dominarla jamás.
Acude a mis hermanos menores,
que ellos seguramente te ayudarán".

Xhuwan se fue en busca de los k'uh
que por el lado norte cuidan al pueblo.
Éstos eran Saj Tanhnaj Oy, Tzulb'al

y Yoq'ob' Hos (bócio de huevo),
y como su extraño nombre lo indica,
Yoq'ob' Hos se burló de Xhuwan, diciendo,
"Toma, aquí te entrego mis poderes",
mostrándole un plato con dos huevos.

Desesperado, Xhuwan se dirigió como venado
ante la magnificencia de Q'anil,
el padre k'uh, ubicado a sur del pueblo.
Xhuwan se posó bajo la sombra del k'uh diciendo,
"Padre Q'anil, dame tus poderes".
Q'anil respondió, extrañado,
"Dime, Xhuwan, ¿por qué me pides los poderes?"

"Mañana mis hermanos irán a una guerra
en auxilio de un pueblo oprimido allá lejos,
y como la fama de los guerreros de Xajla'
ha llegado a sus oídos, hoy nos solicitan
a combatir al enemigo que usa armas extrañas
y que pelea dentro del mar, bajo las olas.
Pero el batallón compuesto de brujos,
¿qué podrá hacer si ellos no son guerreros?
Con ellos, los maleteros moriremos en ese mar
porque únicamente saben transformarse
en feroces animales o en bichos raros
que serán blanco del enemigo desde la playa.

"Por eso, padre Q'anil", volvió a decir Xhuwan,
"quiero ofrecer mi vida por esta gente.
No importa que mi sangre se riegue
y que no vuelva más a esta tierra,
con tal que alcancen la paz y se salven.
Así quiero perpetuar el nombre de este pueblo.
Dame pues ese poder que necesito y anhelo
para partir mañana al salir el gran lucero".

Al escuchar este conmovedor relato,
el buen k'uh respondió, diciendo,
"¿Estás dispuesto a abandonar lo que tienes
y ya nunca volver a tu pueblo
ni arrepentirte después de tener los poderes?"
"Ya he decidido eso antes", dijo Xhuwan.
"Entonces acuéstate y te daré mis poderes".

Xhuwan se acostó, y en esos momentos hubo
un gran trueno y muchos relámpagos
que incendiaban el cielo oscurecido.
La voz de Q'anil se escuchó a través del rayo,
"Levántate y ponte esta camisa amarilla
la cual contiene el poder deseado".
Mientras Q'anil hablaba,
Xhuwan se levantó y se frotó las manos,
lleno de satisfacción.

siete

Cuando Xhuwan regresó precipitado al poblado,
ya se veían en las casas muchas luces
encendidas de los ocotes crepitantes.
Casi llorando, se despidió de sus padres,
de sus hermanos, hermanas y familiares.
Sólo él sabía que el viaje era definitivo
y que ya nunca más volvería a verlos.

Los brujos llegaron a la plaza bostezando
y aventando sus maletas sobre el suelo.
Luego gritaban como grandes señorones:
"¿Dónde están los mozos maleteros?
Pronto, desenreden estos revoltijos".

La expedición se movilizó en la oscuridad
bajo las últimas bendiciones de Jich Mam.

Ancianos, mujeres y niños gemían
mientras nuestros valientes guerreros
gallardamente comenzaron a caminar.

Los viajeros se internaron en la montaña,
iluminados por las luciérnagas que se apagaban
y se encendían juguetonas en sus caminos
como pequeñas estrellas bajo sus pies.
Los maleteros de vez en cuando se detenían
a remover sus mecapales cuando sentían
la mollera hundida o la espalda acalambrada,
mientras los brujos a grandes voces hablaban,
mirando con desprecio a los cargadores
y creyéndose ellos los mejores.

Xhuwan, con la pesada carga sobre la espalda,
callaba sus secretos y ocultaba sus poderes.
¿Quién sabía que ahí caminaba un k'uh
con sus poderes y sus rayos destructores?

A cada tramo, los peligros les acechaban.
Lobos hambrientos atacaban a los maleteros,
que cansados caminaban en retaguardia,
y los que llevaban la delantera, zarzas
y culebras venenosas les salían al paso.
Pero firmes seguían, ya bajo un sol ardiente,
ya bajo lluvias torrenciales que los agotaban.
Su camino por barrancas y montes estaba trazado,
y no se detenían aunque la muerte les estorbaba,
lanzándoles piedras y frutas desde los árboles,
como si imitara a los micos chillones.

ocho

En el lugar de Tenb'al May en los Cuchumatanes,
los brujos ordenaron descansar y ahí acampar.

Sus pescuezudos tecomates estaban vacíos,
y sin el agua no podían batir en sus jícaras
sus sabrosos posoles de masa con cacao.

"Maleteros", dijeron los brujos jactanciosos,
"nosotros estamos hambrientos y con sed.
Irán pues ustedes a traernos el agua
allá en la pinada donde está el nacimiento.
¡Rápido!" dijeron, aventando salivazos al suelo.

"El agua está cerca; iré solo", dijo Xhuwan.
"Yo iré contigo", dijo el otro compañero.
(Éste es a quien llamamos Juan Méndez.)

Mientras iban en camino del ojo de agua,
el compañero de Xhuwan dijo tartamudeando,
"¡Ojalá pudiéramos evitar la muerte segura
adonde caminan ciegos estos brujos vanidosos!"
"Sí, se puede", dijo Xhuwan de inmediato.
"¿Estarías dispuesto a abandonar a tus padres,
a tus hermanos, hermanas y todo cuanto tienes
si se lograran cumplir tus anhelos?"

"Sí, estoy dispuesto", contestó el compañero.
"Bien", dijo Xhuwan. "Tendré un compañero.
Acuéstate sobre el suelo boca arriba,
y yo pasaré sobre ti tres veces".

Tres veces pasó Xhuwan sobre su compañero,
y al terminar la extraña ceremonia,
se irguió el maletero y Xhuwan le señaló,
"Mira ese enorme pino; yo lo derribaré".
Diciendo ésto, Xhuwan tensó sus músculos
y dando un brinco, iluminó el ambiente
con un relámpago que encegu
eció al otro.
Asombrado, Juan Méndez se tapó los oídos,

evitando el trueno que estalló de repente.
Luego un terrible rayo partió en dos piezas
el árbol, desde su copa hasta sus raíces,
ardiendo pronto un fuego inapagable
en la trementina de su añeja corteza.

Cuando el maletero abrió sus ojos,
Xhuwan ya estaba a su lado, mirando el fuego
como si nada hubiera pasado.
"Éste es nuestro poder. Ahora prueba lo tuyo",
dijo Xhuwan al incrédulo compañero.
Sin decir nada, tensó sus músculos
y dio el salto que produjo el relámpago,
luego el trueno y un rayo aterrador
apuntó hacia otro enorme pino.
Pero el ensayo no resultó bien porque Juan
quedó aprisionado en la rajadura del tronco.
Viendo ésto, Xhuwan volvió a transformarse,
y brilló en el cielo un fulminante rayo
que hizo volar en pedazos el gran árbol.

"Ensayemos de nuevo", dijo Xhuwan.
Esta vez, como una furiosa tempestad,
el aprendiz hizo pedazos varios árboles.
"¡Bien hecho!" exclamó Xhuwan emocionado.
"Ahora plantaré más árboles por los cortados".
Diciendo ésto, como serpiente de fuego
cortó las copas de los árboles caídos
y luego las sembró en el bosque como nuevos.

Mientras ensayaban, una fina llovizna
comenzó a caer del cielo azul y despejado.
Presurosos, llenaron sus grandes tecomates
y en silencio regresaron al campamento.
De regreso, Xhuwan previno a su amigo
que no dijera nada a los brujos maliciosos

porque entonces podrían enojarse mucho
y causarles disgustos en el camino.

nueve

Cuando los maleteros llegaron de regreso,
los agitados brujos de ojos de tecolote,
se disputaban aquel repentino suceso:

"¿Oyeron eso?" decía uno. "Nadie como yo puede
provocar el relámpago, el rayo ni el trueno
y hacer que llueva en un cielo despejado".
"Mentiras", dijo otro. "Tú no has hecho eso,
sólo yo tengo esos grandes poderes".

Xhuwan callaba, sólo su corazón se reía, viéndolos atribuirse
poderes que no tenían.

Luego los brujos, con regaños les dijeron,
"¿Por qué se han tardado tanto ustedes?
¿Acaso el agua estaba muy lejos en el cerro?"

Pero como entre ellos había dos *ahb'e* (adivinos), pronto se
dieron cuenta que los dos maleteros eran los causantes de
aquellos trastornos naturales.

Fue así que uno de ellos dijo de pronto,
"De aquí en adelante ustedes dos
ya no cargarán más maletas en sus espaldas".
"Cada quien cargará con lo suyo", dijo otro.
Los otros se callaron al escuchar aquello.
No podían creer que los humildes maleteros
poseyeran la fuerza que estalla en el cielo.

Se miraron los unos a los otros
y reconocieron que nadie entre ellos

tenía esos poderes de fuego en sus manos.
De esta forma cada quien cargó con lo suyo,
y siguieron su camino por montes,
valles y pantanos durante varios días
hasta que al fin llegaron al mar.

No cuentan los ancestros cómo cruzaron,
pero siguen narrando así la escena del combate:
Muchos hombres muertos estaban regados
como conchas a lo largo de la playa,
y por todos lados se veían esparcidos
los arcos rotos y los escudos olvidados.
Al ver ésto, los brujos palidecieron
y retrocedieron con el corazón amedrentado,
prefiriendo mejor volver a casa.

Los brujos decían con mucha preocupación,
"Nosotros podemos pelear como hombres
e incluso convertidos en animales,
pero también como hombres o como animales
nos podrán vencer y dar muerte fácilmente".
Xhuwan y su amigo dijeron que no volverían.
Ellos jamás huirían ni de la muerte misma.
"Jich Mam nos ha enviado", dijo Xhuwan,
"y si huimos de aquí, deshonraremos a Xajla'".
Poco después, con sus maletas en la espalda,
se presentaron nuestros guerreros,
decepcionando al rey que los vio llegar.

"¿Qué clase de burla es ésta?" exclamó el rey.
"Esos muertos allá, picoteados por aves,
formaban un ejército de buenos guerreros.
¿Cómo es que unos pocos descalzos maleteros
vienen hoy ante mí, sin armas y dialogando
en un idioma que no habíamos oído antes?
¿O acaso han venido a insultarme?"

Los de Xajla' no le hicieron caso al rey
y leyendo en su cara sus pensamientos
prestos le respondieron, "Venimos a luchar".

El rey los apartó, sonriendo con angustia.
"Pobres de ustedes, vuelvan mejor a su hogar,
ya que no podrán poner ni un pie en la playa".

diez

Los nuestros dijeron, enardecidos,
"Desde que salimos de Xajla' hace muchos días
hemos venido padeciendo en el camino;
y si hemos cruzado montes, valles y mares
es porque hemos aceptado la invitación
de ofrendar nuestras vidas en esta guerra.
No hemos venido a llorar por los muertos
y retornar a casa como simples caminantes.
Muéstrennos al enemigo y déjennos luchar".

"¿Cómo? ¿Dejarlos combatir para sólo morir?
¿Y podrán ustedes pocos contra un ejército?
¡Vaya si están locos!" replicó el rey.

El rey envió a cuatro guerreros a la playa
para descubrir al enemigo debajo de las olas.
Muy pronto éstos volvieron malheridos
y con la cara y el cuerpo sangrando.
"¡Ya ven, estamos perdidos!" gritó el rey.
"Y si ustedes como locos desean morir,
sacrifíquense, ya que nosotros aquí,
suficientes muertos tenemos a enterrar".

A ésto, Xhuwan se paró y dijo a los brujos,
"Hermanos, ¿podrá la culebra, el gato,
el mico, el jaguar y el sapo

hacer algo en esta guerra que nos toca?
¡Oh no! Se sabrá entonces que nuestro pueblo
envió solamente ridículos y no peleadores.
Retírense a un lugar seguro junto al rey
y dejen a nosotros dos comenzar,
porque somos hoy la única esperanza".
Los dos maleteros caminaron al mar risueños.
Estaban por iniciar el combate
cuando alguien sonriendo se presentó, diciendo,
"Yo soy el hermano de Chiapas. En sueños
supe de la misión, y estoy aquí para ayudar.
Permítanme, entonces, actuar primero".

Entonces en el cielo brilló un relámpago,
luego el trueno y el rayo que cayó al mar,
sacudiendo sus olas y descubriendo al enemigo.
Detrás siguió Xhuwan y el otro con furia.
Una y otra vez descargaron sus rayos,
batiendo las olas ensangrentadas del mar.

Repentinamente apareció el rey en la vega,
vociferando sobre el ruido del combate,
"¡Deténganse! Dejen alguna semilla de ellos.
Ellos son dueños de una gran cultura
y finos fabricantes de hermosas sedas".

Xhuwan respondió, "¿Hemos venido de tan lejos
para no acabar con todos estos demonios?
Bueno, usted es el rey y que se haga su voluntad,
pero en Oxlanh B'en, cuando estalle la guerra,
nosotros mismos regresaremos como ahora,
y nadie más actuará en nuestro lugar.
Entonces, terminaremos con todo el enemigo".

El rey, satisfecho, llamó desde las dunas
a los pocos enemigos que habían quedado vivos

y que salieron del agua con banderas blancas, diciendo,
"¡Piedad! Los nuestros han depuesto su furia,
y hoy venimos derrotados a esta ribera".

El rey decía, dando brincos de alegría,
"En un tiempo Xajla' nutría nuestros sueños,
y he aquí que este puñado de guerreros
lo confirma todo ante nuestra incredulidad.
Fue un error pensar que estos hombres
simplemente venían como tontos a morir.
Ahora su coraje nos lleva a la realidad,
cambiando nuestra derrota en victoria.
Haremos, pues, una fiesta durante tres días,
y les daremos los más altos honores de la corte
y los regalos y tributos que se merecen".

A ésto, nuestros guerreros respondieron,
"No se preocupen en nada por nosotros;
sólo hemos cumplido con nuestra misión
y ahora preferimos regresar pronto
al lejano lugar de nuestro origen".

Así rechazaron los guerreros los tributos,
prefiriendo la paz de la humildad
a cambio de los honores y placeres del mundo.

once

Nuestros abuelos aun murmuran entre dientes
de aquel retorno conmovedor de los vencedores,
pero también guardan como un pesado secreto
el nombre del lugar adonde han ido
y la forma cómo cruzaron el anchuroso mar.

Continúan los abuelos contando que:
Cuando los guerreros avanzaban hacia Xajla',

Xhuwan y su compañero les dijeron a los otros,
"Ustedes pueden volver a Xajla' sin nosotros.
Nosotros que hicimos esa gran matanza
ya no somos iguales a la gente del pueblo,
y ya hemos jurado nunca volver a Xajla'
ni a ver a nuestras propias familias.

"Sólo digan ustedes que estamos con vida
y que nuestros poderes nos evitan volver.
Nos ocultaremos con nuestras flechas doradas
al sur del pueblo, en el monte de Q'anil,
que es casa del padre que nos dio el poder,
y desde ahí cuidaremos a Xajla' del peligro,
elevando nuestras insignias en las nubes
y en el viento el trueno de nuestra voz.
Así estaremos con ustedes para siempre".

Los brujos finalizaron la gran jornada
llorando y moqueando tristemente,
como niños que perdían a sus padres
o como perros que perdían a sus dueños.
La noticia de su llegada regocijó a la gente de Xajla',
quienes salieron a encontrarlos por veredas,
rodeándolos pronto con mucha algarabía,
porque nadie había muerto en campos extraños.

De pronto alguien contó veintiocho hombres.
Todos contaron con dedos de pies y manos,
y faltaban dos. ¡Los dos maleteros!
"¿Dónde están? ¿O acaso habían sido muertos?"

Entonces, los brujos de ojos de tecolote,
tomando aliento, respondieron así:
"Vencimos, vencimos; es nuestra la victoria
gracias a los maleteros y al hermano de Chiapas
(el hombre rayo llamado Juan Carmelo).

Ellos no pudieron regresar con nosotros,
pero desde ahora vivirán en el monte Q'anil,
muy cerca del pueblo. Ellos ya son k'uh,
hombres rayos, cuidadores de Xajla' y Chiapas,
y de quienes debemos estar orgullosos.
Ya no son como nosotros, ya son diferentes,
pero aun así, seguimos siendo de ellos.
Desde la punta del monte Q'anil nos cuidarán
y nos protegerán con sus quemantes rayos.
Así lo prometieron y así lo cumplirán".

Las familias de los héroes se enorgullecieron
y recibieron honores como hijos privilegiados
a través de lo cual fueron olvidando su pesar.
Jich Mam hizo celebraciones en la plaza
mientras una comisión de expertos rezadores
ascendía al volcán de la guerra, el Q'anil,
a sacrificar pavos y quemar candelas y copal
en honor de estos nuevos héroes de Xajla'.

Allá arriba en la punta del Q'anil,
sin que se vea, se siente que respiran,
se siente que ellos viven y hablan;
y sólo cuando hay peligros en las tormentas
o cuando venenosas serpientes nos acechan
en los gruesos troncos de los árboles,
entonces ellos lanzan sus rayos,
alejando el mal que demanda nuestras vidas.

Todo esto creían y relataban los abuelos
con dolorosas remembranzas del pasado,
y así lo han transmitido a sus hijos
y a los hijos de sus hijos, sus generaciones,
hasta llegar a nosotros sus descendientes
que vivimos hoy en Xajla', Jacaltenango.

Komam Q'anil: Ya' k'uh winaj

Komam Q'anil: Ya' k'uh winaj

Yichob'anil

Chin ayb'ailan, sk'atanh ha' Nimam Yax Ha',
kat wichikoj hin t'inhb'an yichob'anil hin konhob'an
haxkam hat b'ay titnajti wik'alan,
b'oj yik'al sunil yuninal konhob' ti'.
Yaj b'ab'el, chin tx'ah hin sat b'oj hin q'ab'
xol sujuyal stz'inanil syaxil q'inal,
katxin hin linhb'an hin b'a,
yuhin q'axpon hune' b'eh k'ayb'alk'ule,
sb'elen heb'ya' paywinaj itzitzal yeyi
yaj ewan b'ay ayah, haka ha'ha' yul tx'otx'otx'.

Walinanxin, chin matz'lihaytoj sti' pahaw,
yib'an syaxtz'ani ha' Niman Yax Ha' ti',
makatoh chin nhus hinpom b'oj no' k'ej haq'b'al
xhchunkul hune' witz yet howalyeh ti',
kathin q'anni haka sq'anni nixhtej hunin
tatoh syeh sb'a heb'ya' k'uh winaj,
heb'ya' mach mak xhk'ojikoj yinh
yet chu howal b'ay xhmaltoj chik' payxah.

¿Matoh aymak mat ohtajnhenoj
hantaj sowal yip sq'aq'al
heb'naj ah Mayab', ah Xajla' ti'?

Waltinanh, ha'un no' usmij choq' yanma
yu hune' tz'ayik b'ay xmaltoj chik', payxatu'
yet xul heb'naj wes, heb'naj kaxhlanh
xelq'ankaniloj heb'naj xtx'otx' Jich Mam
b'ay xhmunlayi, b'ay swatx'e yawal.

¡Ay! kaw mach komay jatut tinanh
haka' smay heb'ya' payat smameal konhob',

heb'ya' winaj ay smay, heb'ya' k'uh winaj,
heb'ya' xmunlayi xanikan hune' b'elen
sajnhen q'inal yul yanma aq'b'al mach stanhb'al.
Xanipaxkan heb'ya' hune' sk'ulch'anil jet
b'ay xaycha no' chik, b'ay ch'awteli no muk',
no' chonh waytzenok'oj hak'a heb'ix q'opoh mach smul,
haktu'pax xin no' hoh ch'ok',
no' k'ej inh ch'ik ilom sat yib'anh q'inal, ·
no' xhalni tet asun tatoh ch'ay ha' nhab'.

Yaj walxin, haka hune' payxa mach stanhb'al
yet xanikoj heb'ya' ninhq'omlom xahanb'al
kaw xoche heb'ya' yahaw Satkanh;
xhwoche hin q'ahb'a'pax yitz'atil hin wi'an
katxin stit txoltxon hune' ik'ti' ti' yulhin nab'alan,
yunheb'al yahwanoj, kat yahlinhnoj
heb'ya' ah Xajla' anhekanoj smay konhob'
yu hune' payat ik'ti' kaw ay sq'aq'al ti'.
Chin q'ahb'a tet ya' B'alunh Q'ana', ya' b'ab'el mameh,
b'oj yinh sb'i ya' Imox, ya' b'ab'el mi'eh,
tet heb'ya' chin q'ahb'a hin xahanb'alan
yunheb'al siq'ni heb'ya' xuq'al sam
sunil te' lob'eal kaw chi' cha' sat hune' tx'otx'otx'
kaw saq'al, Xajla' sb'i ti'.

hune'

Heb'ya' icham winaj xhalni b'ojxin kaw ko sat ch'ilnih
tatoh sunil witz hoynhe konhob' Xajla' ti' kaw saq'al syaxil
haka ch'en stonh ya' b'ab'el komam, B'alunh Q'ana'.
Hakpaxtu' ha' niman sat ko tx'otx' ti',
kaw yaxhnhe tz'antz'o ha', hakatik'a yelaw yuwe ya' Jich Mi'.
B'alunh Q'ana' b'oj Imox sb'ih heb'ya', b'ay titnaj jik'alil.
Heb'ya' hoynhekanoj tx'otx'otx' kaw yax sat b'ay chonh
munlayih, xkonhxin syenikan heb'ya' yinh aq'ankulal
tzet chu ko munlanhen tx'otx', b'oj tzet chu ko tz'unni

jawal; ixim saj sat b'oj ixim q'an sat.
Haktu'xin xu skan xhchik'il heb'ya' jetoj,
xa'ni heb'ya' yipal sq'in ko pixan
haka no' b'alam, b'oj no' q'an tz'ib' b'alam.
Xkonh syenipax heb'ya' tzet chu ko kolnoj kob'a tet howal,
yu ko tanhen hantaj tzet ab'ilkanoj jet:
sunil hej witz ak'al, ha' niman, ko tx'otx',
jawalb'al; ko tiyoxh, jixal;
b'ojxin sunil k'ahole, kutz'ineh.

Hayonhti' xkonyal heb'ya' yuninaloj, xkonhxin syenikanoj
heb'ya' yinh stz'ajanil sk'ul, b'oj yitz'atil swi'.
Haktu'xin xu ko kuynikanoj tzet chu ko watx'en te' b'ok'wi'eh,
b'oj tzet chu ko watx'en ko xanhab'
yinh stz'umal no' sajcheh.

Haktu' xin xu xtxayelax sq'ab' heb'ya' ix yu xhchemlih,
swatx'en heb'ya' q'apq'apeh, chanhe, sintahe, b'oj k'ap koleh;
haktu'xin chu swatx'en heb'ya' sunil xilkok'ap,
katxin yanikoj heb'ya' yelaw q'ap
yu te' hikilit, maka toh schik'il te' hox.

Hakpaxtu'xin xu ko kuyni ko tz'ajni tx'otx' tx'otx',
yu ko tz'ajni ko netb'al: tx'otx' choq',
tx'otx' xih, tx'otx' sek', b'oj tx'otx' sam.

Wal heb'ya' tz'ajan sk'ul xin,
xkonh syepaxtoj heb'ya' tzet chu ko b'isni yoj tz'ayik
b'ojxin tzet chu ko txumni stz'ib' heb'ya' paywinaj
tz'ujb'ilkankoj yinhlaj sk'ul hej ch'en ch'en.

Wal ko melyu xin, te' kakaw;
kaw k'ul chu skoh te', kat yalaxkoj te' xol q'oye
kat juk'ni yal iximal yul te' tzimah kaw stz'uylah yinh
haka kaw stiri yim heb'ix q'opotaj.

Xko kuynipaxoj tzet chu ko txumni tzet yekanoj satyib'anh
q'inal, b'oj tzet chu ko b'isni tz'ayik, x'ahaw,
b'oj hab'il ch'ek'antoj yib'anh ko q'inal.
Haktu' xin chu ko txumniloj yinh sb'elen tx'umel,
naj tz'ayik k'ul b'oj naj xtx'ojal, haxkam wal heb'ya' skolomal jet,
tonhetik'a tzujan heb'ya' jinh, yu honh skolni yinh ko munil,
maka honh skolni tet howal, b'oj tet heb'naj tx'oj yanma.

kab'

Hunun tz'ayik yet xhk'ejb'itoj,
yet stoh tz'ayik yintaj witz nahatlaj,
hatu' yet snanitij heb'ya' icham winaj
yitz'atil stzoti' ya' Jich Mam,
ya' b'ab'el Mame, smam heb' komam:

"Sunil tzet x'ek'toj yib'anh ko q'inal ha' ch'inikanh yip ko pixan
yib'anh hune' b'eh ojlen ti'xin chonh b'elwih
yinh aq'ank'ulal, yunhetik'a ayb'aq'inh xhjetnekanoj hantajtik'a
yik'ti'al ko konhob' ewanto ye yinh ko sat ti'.
Mach mak xhko chakanoj yinhtajil
yunhetik'a yaman ko b'elwiwej".

Haktu' xin xu yalnikan heb'ya' yik'ti'al ko konhob',
nixhtej tzoti' kaw ay smay, yu yok yip ko spixan.
Makatohxin oq'ilal ch'ok yinh janma yet kaw b'iskulal
yalnikan heb'ya' hunq'ahan ik'ti' mach stanhb'al:
Yet xkajtzakanh sk'ul heb'ya' yib'anh q'inal, xanikantij heb'ya'
hune' k'ayilal b'ay x'ay q'aq'a' b'oj q'ol yib'an sunil hej konhob',
haktu' yin xu sujikanojkanh ch'en ch'en
haka ichamtaj yojech kaw kajxanhe nhatxnho
xpaq'chankantoj sunil ichamtaj payat tiyoxh.
Walpax heb'ya' nawal, b'oj heb'ya' tz'ajan sk'ul,
kochxanhe ichamtaj ponhom, maka no' b'ah xu skolnikaniktoj sb'a,
yulaj nhach'en, b'ay xkamkaniktoj
sk'atanh nixhtej xih, sam, b'oj xtxahb'al.

Sunil heb'naj swi'al konhob' x'oq' yilni tzet xu sk'ayiloj
sunil ichamtaj konhob' kaw q'alom.
Haktu' xin xu skankan nhab'en nha tu',
xkonh pujnakanojkan ko sayni hunujxa tx'otx'al
kaw yax sat b'ay chu yayojpaxoj konhob' hunekxa.
Mat suniloj heb'ya' jahaw tu' tzalalal yeyi',
haxkam kaw haytij sowal heb'ya', xhpitz'ni hatxulwuj sb'a heb'ya'
yul te' kakaxhte', b'oj yul te' k'ot.

Haxtu'xin xu spujnakanokanh jet konhob',
nanan xu saynikanoj b'ayxka stoyih.
Aymak xpujnatoj xol k'eb'taj,
aymak xq'axponiktoj ha' nimejtaj ha'.

Hayeb'tam nhab'ilal x'ek'kantoj yib'an anma b'elwom tu'
yet aytokoj sayni b'ay ch'apnoj xolaj q'eb'taj.
Haktuxin xu yapni jet konhob' b'et Ajul
b'ay slahsatnhe sb'a heb'ya' swi'al konhob' skankanoj.

B'etu'xin x'ok munil stzelax ch'en xaj
x'oknikoj ahb'al nhail, yuxinxin Xajla'
x'okkanoj sb'ihoj konhob' tu'.

Yaj wal heb'ya' tz'ajan sk'ul,
sunilnhetik'a tzet chu sk'alni, spuhni, maka suchantoj,
pettik'a syehna heb' y'a b'eh yu sk'ojoch,
xalni heb'ya' tatoh mat k'uluj yok konhob' b'et Ajul tu',
haxkam wal heb'ya' skolomal jet ijb'il b'oj chelb'il yu konhob',
maxhtohab' pax sjel heb'ya' yul snuj sta'wen skani.

Haktu'xin xu yok tzujnoj heb'ya' swi'al konhob' yinh stzoti'
heb'ya' tz'ajan sk'ul, x'okpax b'el yu heb'ya' xol q'eb'taj
k'untik'a stihk'otoj sikilal heb'ya' skolomal jet, i'om b'eh,
yab'en xaycha no' ch'el,
b'oj yilni smaxli no' max sti'laj b'eh.
Kaw nahatil x'ek' heb'ya' b'et Meste'.

B'eti'xin, tolob' ya' Jich Mam hab' sajachnhen
te' ni'an sk'ojoch yul sq'ab',
haktu' hab'xin xu stit lelon te' haka sirwi no' kuwis,
xq'axponik'toj te' yib'an ha' Niman, masanta xk'aykanay te'
yinh sat heb'ya' xol q'eb'taj.
Hab' kaw xk'ay sk'ul heb'ya' swi'al konhob'
x'apni heb'ya' yilnoj b'ay x'ay te' ni'an tz'it te' tu'.
Tolob' kaw k'ulch'an hune' tx'otx'ox kaw q'eb'tajlaj tu',
kaw ayab' no ch'ik b'oj no' stelajil txitam hab' ch'apni
uk'u' ha' b'et ha' snuq' ha' xhal-lax:
Ya' Smij (ya' usmij),
Ya' Hol (ya' holom),
Sti' Ha' Pop.
Wal b'ay xmujitoj te' tz'it te' tu'xin
tolob' kaw saq'al hun ni'an ha'ha' xpitzk'akanh
x'ichikoj sb'elwi hab' ha' masanta sat pahaw
b'ay ay yojomal ha' Niman Yax Ha'.
Haktu' hab'xin xu stzalakanh heb'ya' komam tu'
yalni hab' heb'ya', "¡Ha' tx'otx', ha' tx'otx'!"
yuxinxin Ha' Tx'otx' x'ok sb'ioj hune' ha' ni'an snuq' ha' tu'.

Haktu'xin xu smunlatij ya' Jich Mam tu',
b'oj sunil heb'ya' smamel konhob' tzujan,
stz'unnikan heb'ya' xe'al konhob'
haka smay jilni Sat B'ak'ul (b'ay xpitzk'atij ha' Niman),
b'oj b'ay xjil stit ha' nhab' sat pahaw haka yal sat,
maka yoq'il heb'ya' paywinaj.

Wal ya' Jich Mam tu'xin xab'etoj ya' stzoti' Komam Yahaw
Yib'anh Q'inal, soynikanoj ya' ko konhob' yu heb'naj k'uh,
heb'ya' yib'anh q'inal, skolomal jet,
kaw yilal xhko natij hunun ora, hunun tz'ayik,
b'oj sunil yulb'al hab'il.

Haktu'xin xu xtxolb'alax heb'ya' k'uh sunil soyanil ko konhob':
Ya' B'alunh Q'ana' tu' hat xkan ya' Sat B'ak'ul,

okilb'a, b'ay ch'ok tz'ayik kat sajb'iloj yib'anh q'inal.
Nixhtejalxin, xtxoli heb'naj yaq'b'il:
Naj Ochewal, Wiho, Wamu',
Sipoh, Q'anil Tx'otx', Yoq'ob' Hos, Kaj Icham,
Tzulb'al, Sat Tonhko', Swi' K'ej B'atz', Mapil Ch'en,
Yahb'al Kaq'e', Saj Tanhnaj Oy, Kaje,
Yinh Ch'en, Tx'ej Tunuk, Kulus Wakax,
Witenam, Nilq'o', Nhulnhulwi', K'ajb'al Txoh;
staq'b'al naj Q'anil (skab' smameal konhob').
Haktu'xin xu soychakanoj konhob' ti' yu heb'ya' yib'anh q'inal,
skolomal jet, haxkam heb'ya' xhtanhenoj Xajla' ti';
tx'otx' Niman Konhob' Jacaltenango sb'i
sik'leb'ilkaniloj yu Komam Yahaw Yib'an Q'inal.

oxeb'

Yehb'altohxin yalni heb'ya' icham winaj tatoh:
Walonhti' tz'ajan lahan jekanoj, haxkam b'ab'el Jich Mam
b'oj Jich Mi' xkonh kuynikanoj yinh kaw k'ul.
Heb'ya' xkonh kuyni ko k'enhni te' son, te' akte' b'oj te' su'.
Konh skuynipax heb'ya' koh kanhalwi,
katxin ko b'itnenhtoj ko tzatalal, maka toh ko b'isk'ulal
hakatik'a yalnikanoj yoq'il no' nixhtej ch'ik.

Aypax xin heb'ya' anhlom kaw k'ul hab'ilkanoj ko xol
yu stanhen heb'ya' anma yul yatut yunheb'al mach naj yab'il
xhulxikoj yinh anma yul ko konhob'.
Hakpaxtu' heb'ya' tz'ajan sk'ul b'oj heb'ya' aytzet yohtaj
pettik'a stihiloj heb'ya' tet anma tatoh ay xtx'ojal
xhtit yib'anh ko konhob'.

Yet payxa tu', kaw ay aq'ank'ulalil haxkam tanheb'ilonh
yu heb'ya' Komam Komi'.
Kaw ay smay heb'ya' yul ko sat
yuxin kaw chonh ayb'ail tet heb'ya'.
Haktu xin chu yek' wisla juh, yinh naj aq'ank'ulal,

haxkam mach mak ch'inihaytij ko k'ul,
haxkam mach mak chonh anihay b'ail.
Haxkam lahanonh ko hunil b'ojxin hunenhe ch'imal te'
ayatoj swi' jatut ko hunil.

Yaj wal hune' tz'ayikalxin, kaw janma xhalnian
tatoh ay hune' xtx'ojal chuloj ko xolan.
Somanta xtxikin anma x'okanoj paynoj sq'aq'al,
hakatik'a xtxikin tx'otx' xih lanhan stz'a yib'an q'aq'a'.
Hakpaxtu'xin no' wech, toxanhe mayan yaw no'
skulusnhen no' b'eh yinh ko satan.
Pax no' aq'b'al noq', hununxanhetik'a aq'b'al yoq' no'
kat stzeyen no' stz'ayik jaq'b'alan.

Hank'anhe heb'ya' Komam Komi' ch'ani snimanil ko k'ulan
kat syenitoj heb'ya' yinh smujlub'al
hune' b'eh kaw nahat, haka yetoj tx'umel
b'ay kaw yilal ko b'elwotojan
yunheb'al janokanoj yechel jojlennan.

Haxkamixin kaw oknajtik'a spixan yuninal Xajla' ti',
kaw yilal ko tanhenni tatoh mach b'aq'in ch'el spixan
ko konhob'. Wal ni'an ko tx'otx'al Xajla'
b'ay xkonh pitzk'ati' xin kaw aytik'a smay payat q'inal tu',
yuxintoh kaw halb'iltik'akanoj tatoh koxoltik'a ch'elotoj
heb'naj xhmaq'nojtanhoj howal.

kanheb'

Wal hune' sk'ejb'alil xin yet ko pax xatij xol ko munilan,
xjab'enan tatoh kaw xikiltaj sq'anh te' tinab',
haktu' xu jok tuknoj jab'enojan tzet chuyih
haxkam ponhanxanhe te' tinab' "¡pom, pom, pom, pom, pom!"
xib'ten te' sk'ul ixaleh b'oj uninaleh.
Somanta te' nha, b'oj naj witz xhta'wih yu sq'anh te'.
"¿Tzettaxka chuyih?" konhchian, xhk'ay kok'ulan,

hato xkonh apni jatutan, hatotu' xjab'enan
tzet yelapnoj ye aw, b'oj ich niman ab'ix tu'.

"Tolob' sunil tzehtaj yul konhob' xhyamikoj
yu yab'en tzet chal ya' Jich Mam,
haxkam xol anma tu' sik'laxojiltoj heb'naj winaj kaw ay yip
b'oj heb'naj kaw how xchik'il,
yu stoj smaq'no tanhoj hune' howal aykoj
kaw nahat, kaw nahat yekaniloj
yinh ko konhob', satajkantoj ha' niman pam".

Yiktajb'al konhob' tu'xin hat xyamikoj sunil ix,
nixhtej unin b'oj heb'ya' icham winaj.
Hab' xayanxanhe anma yilni maktaj sik'lelaxojiltoj
xol anma yu stoh yinh howal tu'.
Kaw xikiltaj hab' xu stzotel ya' Jich Mam tu'
yet x'ichikoj ya' stzotel xol anma
tukankoj yab'en tzet chal ya'.

"Yuninal konhob' Xajla', hexti' kaw ay he may,
ab'ewej hune' tzoti' xhwal te yetti'an:
Kaw oq'ilal ye wanmaan xhwalni te yetan tatoh
sq'axepik'toh ha' niman pam, ay hune' konhob' ayto tzet je b'oj,
kawxin lanhan stanhiloj yu hunxa konhob' skajyat.
Ab'xin yul ha' ha' chahatiq' heb'naj howal,
chanikoj heb'naj ch'en ch'en kaw ay sq'aq'al,
yuxin kaw ayxa anma b'oj konhob' xtanhiloj yu heb'naj.
Haxkamxin sunilxa b'ay nahatlaj xhb'ina sb'ih ko konhob'
yu skanhil yeyih, yuxin tinanh xkonh awtelax yu ko toh
ko yenoj skanhil je tet hune' konhob' chonh awten tu',
katxin ko kolni tet niman huchan aykoj yib'anh tu'.
Iwejtij he yanma te yinh xin, k'ahole, haxkam kaw yilal jiwahoj
yinh hune' howal b'ay xax kaw maltoh chik' tu'".

Haktu' hab'xin xu stzotel ya' Jich Mam tu'
k'untik'a hab' sik'leltoj ya' yu sk'ojoch

sunil heb'naj kawla anma, k'ul yinh howal,
haka heb'naj maq'iltik'a kaw how xhchik'il.

howeb'

Yaj ayab' mak mach xcha swi' yilni heb'; naj sik'lelaxiltoj
xol sunil anma yamankoj hune' sk'ejb'alil tu'.
Haktu'xin xu yapni heb'naj tz'ajan sk'ul,
b'oj heb'naj nawal ohtanhen tzetajet ewanil yeyih
xalni heb'naj tet heb'naj sik'leb'ilxa yu ya' Jich Mam.

"Kanojab' heb'naj sik'leb'ililoj ti' sk'atanh yixal
kanojab' heb'naj yinh aq'ank'ulal stz'unu' yawal.
Haxkam: ¿Tzet chu skolnoj sb'a heb'naj jetb'i ti', kat yihwahoj
heb'naj yib'anhiloj heb'naj ch'a'nihatij howal yul ha' ha',
tatoh naj swinajil b'oj naj skanhil yeh scha sb'a yinh hun howal ti'?
Walonh tzajan ko k'ulan, sunil chu juhan".
Haktu' hab' chu yalni heb'naj, k'untik'a hab'
syeh heb'naj skanhil yeh yinh sat anma:

"Walinti'an, chu hin pak'ih lab'ailan", xhi hun naj.
"Walinan, xwakoj hin b'a nawal misalan", xhi hunxa naj.
Haktuxin xu sta'wikanh heb'naj syamanil:
"Walinan, chu hin pak'ih tz'ib' b'alamilan".
"Walinan, chin pak'ih howla ponhomilan".
"Walinan, chu wanikoj hin b'a howla ch'uchuhalan".
"Walinan, chin ok itz'at wechalan".
"Walinan chin ok howla tx'i'alan".

Haktu'hab' yalni heb'naj, k'untik'a hab' xhpak'ih heb'naj noq'al
yinh sat anma. Ab' toxanhe hab' xhtotx'xihay ichamtaj lab'a,
hayab'xin toxanhe hab' ch'ek tz'itlayi,
maka xhnihla haka' howla tx'i, maka haka' b'alam,
xib'tenkanh heb'naj anma yamankoj matz'loj.
Ah, wal yet payxa tu' sunil tzet hab' ay Xajla' ti'
haxkam kalan ha'un naj matzwalil sajchikoj xol anma

yu yiptzenkoj naj yinh xtx'ojal,
maka swab'antoj naj yul sq'ab' huchan.

Wal ya' Jich Mam xin, ab' xhb'sib'on sk'ul ya'
yilni sunil heb'naj tz'ajan sk'ul tu'.
¿Taxka xhto metzohoj heb'naj itzitzal yul konhob' Xajla' ti'?
Haktu' hab' xin xu ya'ni ya' xtxayeb'al yib'an stz'ayik yaq'b'al
heb'naj sayb'il xu tu'.
Hab' matkaw tx'ialoj hab' heb'naj sayloyih,
aynhem waxajeb'oj skawinaj heb'naj,
yaj kaw sunilab' heb'naj kaw tz'ajan sk'ul
stihniloj sunil tzet ewan yeh yinh sat anma.

"K'uxan jinh hayonhti'an", xhihab' heb'naj,
k'untik'a hab' yek' patxxi heb'naj xol anma, lolo'al.
"Mach hunujxa mak chu slahb'ankoj sb'a jinhan,
haxkam hayonhne chu ja'ni il yila' maktaj chonh anihay b'ailan.
Waltinanh, awejay ko k'amte'an, heb'naj ch'ijnojtoj te' pop,
tx'otx' xi, te' tzuh, b'oj ko pichi'an,
haxkam hayonh kaw ay ko mayti'an
hanhk'anhe jotajb'al ti' xhjijatojan".

Hakti'ab'xin stzotel ichamtaj lolo'la nawal tu',
kochnhetik'a kaw xax i'wah heb'naj chab'e.
Kaw nimej xikiltaj hab' chu yul ek' heb'naj sq'uynihay yijatz,
schilnihay heb'naj yaq'b'il k'amte xhto yalanh ijatz.

"¡Tojin ijom ijatzil tu'an!" xhi naj Xhuwan Q'anil.
Tolob' mat kaw nimej winajiloj hab' naj
yaj kaj chilan hab' chal naj stoh kolwal,
walkam ijo ijatziloj hab'nhe.

"¡Hakinan, chintohan!" xhitij hunxa naj.
"Hakinan, hakinan . . .", xaychakanh hunq'ahanxa heb'naj;
yaj yet hunek tu', ab' kawanhnhe heb'naj sik'lelaxiltoj.
Haktu' hab' xin xu syamq'ohay b'et Xajla' tu'

sunil heb'naj sayb'il xu stoh yinh hune' howal tu'.
Kawanh hab' heb'naj ijom ijatz tu' xtoh xol heb'naj nawal.
Chilan hab' stoh heb'naj stanhtzenoj hune' howal tu',
walkam mat yohtajoj hab' heb'naj b'ayta ch'apnoj heb'naj.

wajeb'

Tolob' mach xway naj Xhuwan hune' aq'b'al tu'
yu sayni tzet chu spahnojiltoj kamikal
b'ay kaw chilan swab'antoj sb'a heb'naj nawal tu'.
Hab' kaw xtxumtxun sk'ul naj Xhuwan tu'
sayni tzet chu spaxojtij heb'naj yinh itzitzal,
kat yilnojpax heb'naj sat yixal b'oj yuninal hunekxah.
B'ojxin tzet chu stz'unnujpax heb'naj yawal
katxin toh smujloj heb'naj yinh yeltich'anil ha' Niman,
b'ojxin sunil yelaw sat yib'anh q'inal soyanil konhob' tu'.

Haktu' xu stoh naj b'et ch'en pahaw Sat B'ak'ul
b'et b'ay ay yehob'al ya' B'alunh Q'ana', ya' b'ab'el k'uh winaj
xhtanhen ko konhob' sunilb'al q'inal,
katxin yah jepna sq'aq'al sk'uhal ya' xol asun,
kat jab'en snhurnhunkankan ya' yulaj witz ak'al
yet spahnitoj ya' huchan t'anhankoj jin yulaj b'eh.

Haktu'hab'xin xu stoh naj Xhuwan aq'b'alil
xb'eytzentoj hab' sb'a naj xhchukil b'et Sat B'ak'ul,
b'ay b'ab'el xhjil yichitij ha' nhab',
yib'anhatoj b'ay xhpitzk'atij snuq' ha' Niman Yax Ha'.

Haktu'xin xu yapni naj Xhuwan yin sat naj k'uh,
sq'anni naj yip sq'aq'al k'uh xhlinhmo xol asun tu'
kat yay tzejna sq'aq'al sat yib'anh tx'otx'otx'.
Xta'wihab'kanh ya' B'alunh Q'ana' xalni hab' ya'.
"Xhuwan, wal hin q'aq'alti'an maq'iltik'a kaw ay yip.
Taj machach k'ojoj ha tanhenoj yul ha q'ab'
katxin ha tanhtzenojiloj sat yib'an q'inal ti'.

Maq'il ha toh b'et elilb'a, tet ho' Kaje,
haxkam q'a paxnaj yip ho' hin satajhan".

Haktu'ab'xin xu spaxtij naj Xhuwan b'et Sat B'ak'ul,
hune' luwar b'ay b'ab'el xhkajponhi yahiloj tz'ayik,
xtohxin naj yinh anhe tet naj Kaje,
naj k'uh chonh tanhen sq'axepal konhob'
b'ay xtoh tz'ayik yet xkejb'itoj.

Haktu'xin xu sq'anni naj Xhuwan sq'aq'al naj k'uh.
"Machoj Xhuwan", xhihab' naj k'uh tu'.
"Hune' kamixhe k'ej aykoj winh ti'an
ha' i'nhe sunil yipal hin q'aq'alan,
yaj walach machach k'ojoj
yinh yip hin q'aq'alan.
As tet heb'ya' wuxhtaj q'a' paxnajan
haxkam wal heb'ya' chu hach skolnoj heb'ya'".

Haktu'xin xu stoh naj Xhuwan yilnoj heb'ya' k'uh
xhtanhen ko konhob' skuenta ahilb'a.
B'etu' ay ya' Tzulb'al, ya' Saj Tanhnaj Oy b'oj ya' Yoq'ob' Hos,
yaj wal ya' Yoq'ob' Hos, kaw etlom tik'a ya' yu sb'i tu',
yuxin x'etli ya' yinh naj Xhuwan, xalni hab' ya':
"Tiyalah, xhwak'oj sunil wip tah wetan", xhi ya' k'uh tu',
syeni ya' sos yinh sat naj Xhuwan.

Haktu'xin xu syajb'iloj sk'ul naj Xhuwan
x'elpax anhe yu naj haka sajche, xtoh naj yalnoj sb'isk'ulal
tet naj Q'anil, naj k'uh chonh tanhen skuenta ek'ilb'a.
Ha' x'apni naj yinh sat naj k'uh, xalni naj:
"Mam Q'anil, a' s'q'aq'al ha wip wetan".
Xtawihab'kanh naj Q'anil:
"¿Tzetyuxin cha q'an sq'aq'al wip ti'an, Xhuwan?"

Xta'wihab' naj Xhuwan:
"Hekal sab' xhtoj heb'naj wuxtaj yinh howalan

yunhe skolnoj heb'naj hune' konhob' lanhan stanhtzelaxiloj,
yaj haxkam nab'iltij sb'ih ko konhob'
yu skanhil yeyi, yuxin tinanh ch'awtelax yuninal konhob'
yu stoh smaq'noj tanhoj hune' howal tu'.
Hab' kaw k'ul xhch'en heb'naj chakoj, b'ojxin hab' yul ha'
eb'ab'il sb'ah heb'naj, cha'nihatij heb'naj howal.
¿Tzetxin chu skolnoj sb'a heb'naj nawal xhtoh yinh howal,
tatoh mat yetwanoj hune' howal ti' yeh heb'naj?
Kaw mach xtxumal ko kamoj yinh heb'najan, haxkam
hanhk'anhe spak'i heb'naj howla noq'al chu yu,
katxin ya'noj kamoj sb'a heb'naj sti' ha' niman pam tu'.

"Yuxin xhwal tawetan mam Q'anil", xhihab' naj Xhuwan tu',
"tatoh xhwa' hin q'inal yu hin kolni wetb'ian.
Mach wok yinhan tatoh xhmalotoj hin chik'ilan,
katxin matxa b'aq'in chin meltzooj sat hin tx'otx'alan,
yaj tahne toh ch'ok naj aq'ank'ulal xol anma.
Xhwochehanxin tatoh xhwa' b'inaoj sb'i ko konhob'an.
Chin q'anan tatoh cha wa' ha q'aq'al tu' wetan, haxkam
hekal ch'eloj b'el wuan, yet ch'ahojiloj naj Saj B'es".

Ha' xab'en naj Q'anil sb'isk'ulal naj Xhuwan xalni hab' naj:
"¿Yelmi cha walah tatoh mach stz'a ha k'ul yinh tzet ayach,
katxin matxa b'aq'in chach meltzo yul ha konhob';
b'oj taj xhkab'konojkanh ha k'ul tzujanxa?"
"Xax kin ok tuknoj hin txumu'an", xhi naj Xhuwan.
"Ayanh hilnoj xin, kat wa'ni hin q'aq'alti' tawetan".

Haktu'ab'xin xu yay hilnoj naj Xhuwan x'ahnahab' jepnoj
kayumpah, xq'anhnahab'kanh naj k'uh.
Ab' sanhanxanhe yek' hab' naj k'uh hune' akb'alil tu'.
Huneptuxin, x'ahab' yaw naj Q'anil, xalni hab' naj:
"Ahanh wanoj, kat ha wanikoj hune' kamixhe q'an tilah
haxkam ha' i'nhe smay hin q'aq'al cha q'anti'an".
K'unti'k'ahab' stzotel naj Q'anil tu', sik'ni sb'a naj Xhuwan.
Hab' kaw stzalalalxa hab' yeh yanma naj.

hujeb'

Yet x'apni naj Xhuwan yinh anhe yul konhob'
hab' niman sahk'alxa hab' yeyi haxkam ayxa hab' b'ay
aykoj q'aq'a yinh te' tah yulaj nha.
Hab' oq'ilal yeh sat naj Xhuwan tu',
xtaq'lihab'kan naj tet smam smi', yuxtaj, b'oj yanab';
haxkam hanhk'anhe hab' naj ohtajnhe tatoh matxa sb'aq'inhaloj
xhpaxotij naj yinh hune' b'el b'ay xhto tu'.

Hab' kaw ch'ahab' xhch'ab'ti' heb'naj nawal tu'
yet x'apni heb'naj b'oj yijatx hune' sahk'al tu'.
Kaw nimej anma hab' chute sb'a heb'naj, sq'anni heb'naj:
"¿B'aytu' ay heb'naj k'amte' ijom ijatz?
Hulujab' heb'naj b'eti' ha'mataj yu sq'uynihay heb'naj ijatz ti' ".

Haktu'hab'xin xu stoh heb'naj b'elwom tu'
xa'nihab'kan ya' Jich Mam tu' xtxayeb'al yib'anh heb'naj.
Sunil hab' icham winaj, ix, b'oj nixhtej hunin hab' ch'oq'ih
yet x'ok b'el yu heb'naj yuninal konhob' kaw kanhye
xtoh yinh hune' howal q'axeptatoj ha' mar tu'.

Haktu' hab' xin xu yok b'el yu heb'naj xol q'eb'taj,
yaj kaw k'ejhab' holo, yuxin tzejlen hab' no' stzujli
kat stanh sq'aq'al yul sb'e heb'naj, haka nixhtej tx'umel hab'
smutz'munay sq'aq'al no' yalanh yoj heb'naj.
Xhchalonhemih katxin xew heb'naj ijom ijatz tu',
kat sek'ni heb'naj spopom yinh swi' yet kaw kanxa stel yichinh
heb'naj yu yalil ijatz. Wal heb'naj nawal xin,
tonhetik'a hab' xhchiwa ay heb'naj smayni heb'naj sk'amte',
haxkam hank'anhe heb'naj kaw winaj yalni.

Wal naj Xhuwan xin, kaw al hab' yijatz naj chab'eh
yaj machab' tzet chal naj tatoh aytzet hab' yohtaj naj.
¿Mak ohtajnhe tatoh hune' naj k'uh winaj, b'oj sunil
sq'aq'al hayab'koj sb'elwi xol heb'naj nawal tu'?

Hab' nanannhe huchanil chil heb'naj yulaj sb'eh,
xhchaloyi, ab' no' oj ch'eltij yinh heb'naj ijom ijatz
haxkam kaw nahat hab' xhkan heb'naj yinh yetb'i.
Wal heb'naj i'om b'eh xin, te' tx'ix maka no' lab'a
kaw how sti' ch'elab'tij lemna yul sb'eh heb'naj.
Yaj machab' chiloj heb'naj sb'eh yinh sk'ul, walkam xol q'a',
maka xol nhab', hab' kaw yilal xhb'elwi heb'naj.
Hune' b'eh satlaj pahaw maka xolaj q'eb'taj b'ay xhb'elwi
heb'naj tu', yetwanoj tik'axa heb'naj yeyih yuxin machab'
slinhb'a sb'a heb'naj, walkam ch'etlikoj naj kamikal
yul sb'eh heb'naj, matoh naj matzwalil xhk'ojwatij yinh heb'naj
haka yetli no' max yet sb'ejnitij no' lob'eal yinh anma.

waxajeb'

Tolob' yet x'apni heb'naj b'et Tenb'al May
xalni hab' heb'naj nawal tu' tatoh xew heb'naj.
Matxa hab' pax ha'ha' yul te' leje tx'inhan snuq' stzuh
tzik'anab' xol smaq'ah heb'naj skakaw yal ixim yalni
toh kaw xa taj xul te' tzimah manh ha'il.

"K'amte' hey, tzab'ex wej", xhihab' heb'naj nawal tu'.
"Walonhti'an kaw chonh nhocha han b'oj xhtaj ko ti'an,
wal tinan, kaw yilal he toh he yi'noj ha'ha'
b'et hune' ha' ni'an snuq' ha' xol tahlaj.
Aswejxin, tinanh nhenayi",
xhihab' heb'naj; xhtajin tzub'lihay heb'naj sat tx'otx'.

"Hayin chin tohan, kawil ay ha'", xhihab' naj Xhuwan.
"Tojin tawinhan", xhihab' hunxa naj ijom ijatz.
(Tolob' ha' naj tu' xhal-lax Xhuwan Mentes-al.)

Yet hayab'koj heb'naj yul b'eh stoh i'oh ha' tu'
yalni hab' naj yetb'i naj Xhuwan tu' tet:
"Oximih chu ko pahnitoj naj kamikal b'ay rinhan sb'elwitoj
ichamtaj kewa' nawal chal sb'a kanhyehal ti'".

"Walxin xhtik'a huyih", xhihab' naj Xhuwan.
"¿Yaj, taxkaxin ch'el yinh ha k'ul ha wanikanoj
ha mam ha mi', ha wanab', ha wuxhtaj, b'oj sunil tzet ayach,
tatoh ch'a'lax tzet cha q'an ti'?"

"Ho', kaw ch'el yinh wanma han", xhihab' naj.
"Kaw k'ul chaltu', ayxa wetb'i tinanhan", xhi naj Xhuwan.
"Hilb'atoj hab'a sat tx'otx', kat hach hin xalb'anojan,
oxel el chin ek'oj ta wib'anhan".

Tolob' oxel el x'ek'toj naj Xhuwan yib'an naj yetb'i tu'.
Ha' yet hab' xtanhk'o heb'naj yuni hune' ewanil tu'xin,
x'ah hab' wanoj naj k'amte' tu', syenitoj hab' naj Xhuwan:
"¿Cha wil hune' te' tah tula? cha wila' k'anab' hin b'ejnok'ojan".
Haktu' hab'xin xu yinitij naj Xhuwan tu' xip
x'ahna hab' jepna k'uh sat kanh, haka kayumpah
xmaq'ni tanhoj smujlub'al naj yetb'i naj tu'.
Kaw xk'ayab' sk'ul naj Xhuwan Mentes tu', smajchen naj xtxikin
yunheb'al mach xhchakanhb'i naj yu sq'anh naj k'uh.
Haktu' hab'xin xu yayna tzejna k'uh yib'an te' tah tu'
xpaxab'nakan silson te', yinh xhchunkul masanta yich xe',
k'untik'a hab' xtzujlinakanh q'a'q'a' mach xhtanhi
yinh sq'olal stajinhal stz'umal te'.

Ha' yet sajnitoj naj ijom ijatz sb'aq' sat
ab' linhanxanak'oj naj Xhuwan sk'atanh naj
yilni yahkanoj xaj q'aq'a yinh te' ich niman tah tu'
haka'tik'a matzet xunapax naj.
"Ha' ti' yip ko pixan tu'. Ilwe ha wet tinanh",
xhihab' naj Xhuwan tet yetb'i tu'.
Machab' tzet chal naj yetb'i naj tu', xilwen hab' sb'a naj.
Hab' x'ahna tz'itna naj haka kayumpah,
salanhlana hab' sat kanh, x'ayna jepna k'uh
yib'anh hunexa te' ich niman tah xol q'eb'taj.
Yaj mat k'ulujhab' x'elkoj hune' ilweb'ail tu'
haxkam xkankan tx'apnoj naj Xhuwan

yul satilal te' ich niman tah tu'.
Ha' xilni naj Xhuwan tatoh tx'oj yekoj yetb'i naj
x'ahnahab' tzejna naj sat kanh, xlinhlana k'u
xmaq'ni pohoj te' ich niman tah b'ay tx'apan yetb'i naj tu'.

"Kam jilweninoxa ko b'a", xhihab' naj Xhuwan.
Walxa yet skayel tu', hab' kochxanhe hunuj k'ayilal
xu yek' jepoh naj lanhan skuyni sb'a tu'
smaq'nikanoj pohoj naj hun tenan te' tah.
"Ha' ti' xhwochean", xhihab' naj Xhuwan.
"Waltinanh, chin ok hin tz'unu' selel te' te'
xko b'ejayoj ti'an".
Hab' kochxanhe q'a' hab' yek' chulchun naj
stzok'niltoj swi' te' ichamtaj tah maq'b'ilk'oj tu'
stz'unnipaxay naj te', yu xhch'ib'kanh te' hunekxa.

Hab' kaw lanhan yilwen sb'a heb'naj, xtitna musmun
ha' nhab', k'am hab' saq'al sajanil satkanh.
Hab' yinhxanhe anhe snotze heb'naj ichamtaj stzuh
xpaxtij heb'naj b'ay aykan heb'naj nawal echmawal.
Yulb'eh hab' tu' xal naj Xhuwan tet yetb'i
tatoh matzet chal naj tet heb'naj nawal tu'
haxkam tatoh machoj, xhtij sowal heb'naj,
katxin yetlojkanh heb'naj yul b'eh.

b'alunheb'

Hab' kaw ayab'kanh howal yu heb'naj nawal tu' chanikoj hab'
heb'naj smay, tatoh heb'naj lanhan hab' smunlayi
yuxin hab' kaw xhq'anh naj k'uh satkanh:

"¿Xe yab'e huntu? mach mak xhk'oji winh hayinti'an katxin
sajchi haka hin sajchi ti'an kat ya'ni ayoj ha' nhab',
walkami mach asun satkanh".
"Leq'ti'ach, tzik'anab' chach okih, to hayinhe ti' ay wohtajb'al
yinh tzetet ewan yeh ti'an".

Hab' machab' tzet chal naj Xhuwan b'oj yetb'i tu'
tonhe hab' stzeb'i heb'naj yilni ichamtaj nawal
chal sb'a winajil tu', k'am machab' tzet yohtaj.

Huneptu', hab' xmaywakanh heb'naj nawal tu':
"¿Tzetyuxin lanhanto he yulih cho'?
¿Tox kaw nahat ay ha'ha' tu' yuxin kaw x'ek' he q'inal?"

Yaja tolob' ayab' kawanh heb'naj ahb'e xol heb'naj
yuxin hab' pet xtxum heb'naj ahb'e tu' tatoh heb'naj
k'amte' tu' hab' ch'uten hune' kayb'al k'uleal tu'.

Haktu' hab'xin xu yalnikanh hune' naj ahb'e tu':
"Waltinanh, hex kamte' hex ti' matxa che yi'atoj ijatz ti'
stel he yichinh".
"Nanan jijnitoj jijatz", xhihab' hunxa naj ahb'e.
Hab' sb'ejnikan heb'naj nawal tu' stzoteli'.
Machab' cha' heb'naj nawal tu' yuluj sk'ul
tatoh heb'naj kawanh k'amte' tu' chu spak'i k'uhal.

Haktu' hab'xin xu sakhen sb'a heb'naj nawal tu' xtxumniloj
hab' heb'naj tatoh machab' mak chuh spak'ih k'uhal
haka heb'naj kawanh k'amte' tu'.
Haktu' hab'xin xu yijnikanh heb'naj yijatz tu'
x'ichihab'koj heb'naj sb'elwi hunekxa xolaj q'eb'taj,
ha'laj, b'oj tajinh witz ak'al;
masanta x'apni heb'naj sti' ha' niman pam (mar).

Matzet chal heb'ya' payat Jich Mam b'oj Jich Mi' tu'
tzet xu yek'toj heb'naj q'axep ha' niman ha' tu',
yaj xhtoh yik'ti'nhetoj heb'ya' tzet xute sb'a howal tu':
Hab' toxanhe hab' tixhantoj kamom haka stixhitoj
no' mik'in sti' ha' mar tu',
hab' nananxanhe hab' b'ay pak'antoj te' tz'it te'
b'oj sunil tzet chakoj heb'naj spahb'aloj yin howal tu'.
Ha' yet xilni heb'naj nawal sunil kamom tu' xin,

hab' kaw xpax heb'naj yinhtajil xiwkilal,
sq'anni hab'toj sb'a heb'naj pax, yatut.

Ha' xilni heb'naj tatoh tx'oj yekoj, xalni hab' heb'naj:
"Walonh ti'an, chu ja'ni howal haka heb'naj winajan,
maka toh chu ko pak'i noq'alan; yaj haka jilni sya'tajil yeh
hun howal ti' walkami anma maka noq' jean,
hab'an chu ko potx'laxojan".
Wal naj Xhuwan xin, machab' tzet chal sk'ul naj b'oj yetb'i,
ni machab' xiw heb'naj tet kamikal tu'.
"Kaw ya' Jich Mam xkonh taq'entij kolwal yinh hun howal ti'
yuxin tatoh chonh elokanh, spixan ko konhob' xji'aloj",
xhihab' naj Xhuwan tet heb'naj nawal tu'.
Hab' ayab'kanh nixhtej yijatz heb'naj stel yichinh
yet x'apni heb'naj syenoj sb'a tet naj rey tu'.
Hab' xyajb'iloj sk'ul naj yet xilni naj jet konhob'.

"¿Tox etal che yu winhan?" xhihab' naj rey tu'.
"Sunil heb'naj kamnajay sti' ha' mar tula kaw sunil heb'naj
k'ul yinh howal, yaj xkam heb'naj.
Waltinanh xin, tzik'anab' chu yi'waoj haywanh heb'naj ijon ijatz,
mach xanhab', b'oj nan yab'xub'al xul ti',
toh mach xhch'en heb'naj chakoj yu skolni sb'a.
¿Matoh tonhe xul heb'naj etloj winhan?"
Tolob' machab' tzet xal heb'naj ah Xajla' tet naj rey tu,
yaj tonhe hab' chab'e heb'naj spohli, naj.
Nixhtejalxin hab' xta'wikanh heb'naj: "Yinh howal chonh hulan".

Hab' b'isk'ulal hab' ye naj rey tu' xalni hab' naj:
"K'anch'anex, maq'il he paxtoj te yatut,
haxkam machex k'ojoj he yanojay he yoj sti' ha' mar tu'".

lahunheb'

Haktu' hab'xin xu yalnikanh heb'naj jet konhob' tu':
"Hatax yet xkonh tit b'et ko konhob' tu'an

kaw ayxa sya'tajil xax jil yulaj b'ehan.
Awteb'ilonh yu ko kolwa yinh hune' howal ti'an
yuxin nahat tx'otx' b'ay xkonh titan, xolaj q'eb'taj,
b'ojxin xkonh q'axpontij ha'ha' b'oj tajin witz ak'alan.
Mat oq'ojojnhe chonh hul yib'an kamoman
kat ko paxtoj b'ayonh haka heb'naj komon b'elwoman.
Yewej jetan b'ay ay heb'naj ch'ani howal tu'
katxin honh he chanikoj yinh hun howal ti'an".

"¿Tzik'anab'i? ¿Matoh che yoche he kam yinh hun howal ti'?
¿Tom chex k'ojoj yinh hun tenan heb'naj a'om howal tu'?
Tita' somchanajkanh yul he wi'", xhihab' naj rey tu'.

Kanhnwanh winaj hab' xtoh syenoj sti ha' mar b'ay eb'ab'il
sb'a heb'naj ch'ani howal yul ha'ha' tu'.
Hab' chik'tajxanhe sat b'oj snimanil heb'naj kanhwanh tu'
yet xmeltzo heb'naj yinh xhchejb'anil.
"Xmameyilxin, tx'ojtik'a jekoj, yaj tatoh che yoche kamoj he b'a,
asi'wej, matxa sje ko k'ul ko muju' yaq'b'il kamoman", xhihab' naj rey tu'.

Haktu' hab'xin xu yalnikanh naj Xhuwan tet yetb'i tu'.
"¿Wuxhtaj, taxkaxin xhk'oji no' lab'a, no' mis, no' max,
no' b'alam, b'oj no' ponhom stanhtzenojayoj hun niman howal
b'ay xkonh tit ti'? ¡Kewa'il hun xhju ti'!
Chim hal-laxoj b'aq'in tatoh kewa' winajnhe
xatij ko konhob' yinh howal.
Waltinanh, hitzanhwejtoj nahat sk'atanh naj rey
kat ko kan ko kawanhil jilwenoj kob'a yinh hun howal ti'an
haxkami jinhxanhe ay kawxob'al k'ulean".
Stzeb'i hab' heb'naj yet xtoh heb'naj sti' ha' mar tu'.
Hab' kaw lanhan hab' yokoj heb'naj yinh howal
yet x'apni lemna hunxa naj winaj tz'ajan sk'ul.
"Wuxhtaj, hayinti' Chapa hinan. Haka'tik'a yul wayike
xu wab'en sq'umal hun howal b'ay kex tit ti'an
yuxin xkin tit kolwalan.
Tinanhxin wilwe' hin b'a b'ab'elan".

Haktu' hab' xu yek'na jepoh kayumpah satkanh
tzujantik'a hab' xu yayna sanhna naj k'uh yul ha' mar
x'ahnakaniloj nhirna heb'naj matzualil tu' hab'an.
Hab' tzujantik'a hab' xu stopax naj Xhuwan b'oj yetb'i.
Hab' tzejoxanhe yay K'uh yul ha' mar tu',
tolob' xkaj ponhikaniloj ha' yu chik'.

Hab' toxanhe ch'el yaw naj rey x'apni naj yih anhe sti' ha' mar,
xalni hab' naj, "Tukb'awej howal, awejkan hunuj yinhatil heb'naj,
haxkam toh ay yohtajb'al heb'naj.
Heb'naj xhwatx'en xilq'ape seda ti', kaw saq'al".

Xta'wi hab'kanh naj Xhuwan, "¿Kaw nahat xkonh titan,
matxin cha je xhtanhiloj sunil heb'naj matzwalil ti'?
Mach xtxumal, yahaw ha weyi, yuhab' tzet chal ha k'ul;
yaj yinhtoh Oxlanh B'en, yet ch'okopax hunxa howal,
hayonhtik'a chonh hulujpaxan,
haxkam match mak cha'a' smay ko helelojan.
Hatomtu' xhko tanhtzeloj sunil heb'naj matzwalil ti'an".

Hab' kaw stzala naj rey, x'awitoj naj tet haywanh heb'naj
matzwalil xkolpa yinh howal tu'.
Haktu' xu yahiloj heb'naj b'oj nixhtej q'ape saj yul sq'ab'
xalni hab' heb'naj:
"Niman che yute he k'ul jinhan, chewb'ojab'ayoj
hun howal ti', okojab' aq'ank'ulal ko xol".

Hab' toxanhe t'ujla yah naj rey tzalalal, xalni hab' naj:
"Payxa, kaw xhtik'a jab'e sb'ina sb'i konhob' Xajla' tu',
waltinanh xin, kaw haywanh winajilalnhe heb'naj xul
a'noj jila' tatoh kaw yeli' aytik'a smay hune' konhob' tu'.
Sukal tik'amih xwalnian, tatoh hunq'ahan heb'naj winaj ti'
kamojnhe chul heb'naj haka anma kewa'.
Waltinan, smay heb'naj xmaq'niltoj hune' huchan ti' jib'an
xinikanh heb'naj ko pixan,
haxkam hayonh xkonh i'wah yinh hun howal ti'.

Kaw yilal ko q'inhnhen oxeb'oj tz'ayikalil,
kat ja'ni okoj spixan hunq'ahan heb'naj winaj ti',
katxin ja'ni hantaj tik'a tzet sq'an sk'ul heb'naj".

Xta'wihab'kanh heb'naj jet konhob' tet naj rey:
"Matzet tx'ial che yakoj yinh he k'ul juan,
tonhe xkonh hul ko yijye' hun ko chejb'anilti'an;
waltinanxin, kachan xtanhk'o hun howal ti',
xhjochean tatoh chon paxtoj sat ko tx'otx'alan".

Tolob' haktu' hab' xu spahnitoj heb'naj jet konhob' tu',
hantaj sq'alomal tzet xallelax tet heb'naj.
Haxkam aq'ank'ulal xoche heb'naj, mataj naj sq'alomal.

hunlanheb'

Yehnhetoh yalni heb'ya' icham winaj yik'ti'al,
tzet xu spaxtij heb'naj jet konhob' xb'eyk'oj yinh hune' howal tu',
yaj machmak ohlajnhe tzet sb'i konhob',
matoh tx'otxotx' b'ay xb'eyk'oj heb'naj yinh howal,
b'ojxin tzet xu sq'axponik'toj heb'naj yib'anh ha' mar.

Chalxin heb'ya' icham winaj jab'e':
Tatoh yet lanhan skawilnikoj heb'naj yinh konhob' Xajla',
xalni hab' naj Xhuwan b'oj yetb'i tet heb'naj nawal tzujan yinh.
"Walexti' chu he meltzo Xajla' he chukil, haxkam hayonh
x'ok ko mul yinh hune' howal tu'an,
matxa jet lahanoj anma ay yul ko konhob'an.
B'ojxin xax jalkanojan tatoh matxa sb'akinhal
chonh meltzo jila' juninal yul ko konhob'an.

"Che yala' tet komam b'oj komi'an tatoh k'ulnhe jean
yaj yu sq'aq'al k'uh ab'il jet ti'an, matxa chu ko meltzoan.
Hat xhko k'ub'akantoj kob'a b'oj ko q'aq'al b'et ek'ilb'a,
swi' naj Q'anil, b'ay ay yatut ya' k'uh x'a'ni jip ti'an.
B'etu'xin xhko tanhetij konhob' tet naj xtx'ojalan

katxin ko yenojan tatoh itzitzal jean yet xhq'anhokanh naj k'uh
xol asun. Haktu'xin chu ko tanhenoj konhob'an,
tinanh, b'oj sunilb'al q'inal mach stanhb'al".

Haktu' hab'xin xu staq'likanoj heb'naj tet hunun,
siq'sonkanokanh heb'naj nawal yoq'ih
haka nixhtej unin k'aynajtoj yinh smam smi',
maka haka yoq' metx tx'i' k'aynajtoj yinh yahaw.
Hab' kaw ay tzalalal yet x'apni sq'umal tatoh
yapnixa heb'naj yul konhob', yuxin sunil anma
xtit chawal yinh heb'naj yul b'eh. Kaw ay tzalalal
haxkam mach heb'naj xkam yinh howal.

Yaj hab' waxajeb' skawinaj nhe heb'naj xmeltzoyi.
Sunil hab' mak xb'isni yiximal sq'ab' b'oj yoj, xnachatij
tatoh kawanhtoh heb'naj matzet. ¡Heb'naj ijom ijatz!
"¿B'aytu' xkan heb'naj? ¿Matoh xkam heb'naj yinh howal?"

Hab' toxanhe xhmutz'la sat heb'naj nawal, haka no' ku noq'
xinitij heb'naj yip xinh, xalnihab'kanh heb'naj:
"Xkonh i'wayi, hayonh xkonh i'wayi, yuch'antiyox tet heb'naj
kawanh xtoh yalanh ijatz, b'oj naj juxtaj ah Chapas
(naj k'uh-winaj xhal-lax Xhuwan Kalmelal).
Yaj matxa xu smeltzo heb'naj jinhan,
wal tinanh hatxa ch'eoj heb'naj swi' naj Q'anil,
skawilal ko konhob'. Haxkam xax pak'i heb'naj k'uhal
yu stanhenoj heb'naj Xajla' ti' b'oj Chapas.
Yuxin kaw yilal ko nanitij heb'naj.
Matxa jet lahanoj heb'naj, nanxa yeh heb'naj,
yaj walonh hunenhetik'a jekoj yinh yanma heb'naj.
Swi'tah naj Q'anil tu' chonh stanhetij heb'naj,
katxin honh stanhenoj heb'naj yu sq'aq'al, haka' k'uh.
Kaw yilalxin syijyenoj heb'naj tzet halb'ilkanoj yu ti'".

Hab' kaw xtzala smam smi' heb'naj kawanh k'uh tu',
haxkam kaw smay konhob' xakoj heb'naj.

Somanta yuninal heb'naj kaw x'alaxkoj spixan,
yu snimannhen sk'ul, kat sk'aynitoj sb'isk'ulal.
Haktu' hab' xu yichi q'inh yu ya' Jich Mam,
k'untik'a hab' xtoh hun majan heb'ya' txahlom
a'okoj haq'b'al, b'oj nhusu' pom swi' naj Q'anil
yinh sb'ih heb'naj kawanh x'anikoj smay konhob'.

Yuxin swi' naj witz Q'anil tu', walkami mach xhjilah,
kaw xhjab'e yi'ni heb'naj saq'oh kat stzotel heb'naj.
Yuxin ta ay naj huchan t'anhantij jinh, haka kaq'e nhab',
maka no' howla lab'a ayiktoj yul sk'ul te' te' honh yechmani,
hato tu' ch'ayoj tzejna heb'naj smaq'noj tanhoj huchan
xhalxikoj sk'ul yinh ko q'inal.

Sunil ti'xin cha' heb'ya' icham winaj yuloj sk'ul
kat yalni heb'ya' jab'e',
haka tik'a hunuj payat tzoti' kaw mach stanhb'al;
haktu'xin chu yik'ti'nhentoj heb'ya' tet yuninal,
b'oj tct sunil syihtxikin, masanta xulkanoj jet,
hayonh yuninal hune' konhob' Xajla' (Jacaltenango) sb'i ti'.

Notes

Author's note: The name "Q'anil" means "yellow power" (from *"q'an,"* "yellow," and the derivative suffix *"-il,"* signifying "related to"). "Q'an" is also the color related to the south, according to the Maya worldview, and is expressed in glyphs and in the ethnohistorical books such as those of the *Chilam Balam.*

Q'anil is the name of one of the seven brothers that founded Xajla', according to the accounts obtained by the anthropologist Juvenal Casaverde in 1973–1974. Q'anil is also one of the four Year Bearers *(Ijom Hab'il),* who alternate, according to the Maya calendar, in the following order: Watanh, Q'anil, Ah, and Chinax (La Farge and Byers 1931, 1997).

El Q'anil is the most important legend of Jakaltek oral tradition. The present work combines various fragments from different sources and narrators. The most important of the elders I interviewed was Antun Luk, who was said to be a descendant of Xhuwan Q'anil, the culture hero of this legend. Antun Luk was about eighty years old when I interviewed him and knew by heart the ceremonial prayers that were recited in couplets, a special characteristic of Maya ceremonial and religious literature. Don Antun Luk was also a wonderful curer, whose specialty was setting broken bones. He died in 1984, when I was still in exile.

Introduction

1. Edmonson (1982), Recinos (1983), Tedlock (1996), and Carmack and Mondloch (1989), among others, have suggested that the Maya documents were hieroglyphic texts earlier, in pre-Hispanic times. When the written tradition of Maya literature and history began to be lost, especially during the Spanish invasion,

what had remained in the oral tradition was compiled in Maya texts but with Latin characters.

2. Recinos (1983) refers to several translations and interpretations of these names in their notes to the first part of the book.

3. This custom of considering thunder and lightning as a sign or portent of future events and for weather forecasting is also found in the *Books of Chilam Balam*. For example:

> The wise men and teachers tell us that when thunder is heard in the east on March 21, it is a sign that in coming years there will be many evils, such as quarrels, misfortunes, and envy. If the thunder is heard in the south or if there is an eclipse of the sun or moon, it is a sign that there will be deadly epidemics throughout the world. . . . If thunder is heard on Saturday, day of the planet Saturn, or if the light of the sun or moon is darkened, it is a sign that there will be two types of misfortunes: great evils among the people and war. (Craine and Reindorp 1979:50–51)

4. When I wrote *El Q'anil* during the 1970s, I did not know of the existence of Oliver La Farge's ethnography about the Jakalteks. This exemplifies one of the problems of anthropology in general, that the ethnographers' works have been written in foreign languages such as English, then published and filed away in libraries abroad. Efforts have not been made to translate the material, at least into Spanish, and repatriate these documents to the communities where the information was gathered. La Farge's work has now been translated into Spanish by Oscar Velázquez and Víctor Montejo and published in Guatemala (1997), thus accomplishing the return of this ethnography to the Jakalteks and the Maya and non-Maya communities of Guatemala.

Pórtico

1. It is customary among indigenous people that, when referring to the ancient stories of the ancestors, the storyteller must commence the narration with a demonstration of respect for their memory. Maya ancestors are remembered with respect and admiration, because they have shown the way that their descendants must follow as true sons and daughters. In other words, it is necessary to remember the founding fathers of the town, in homage to their humanity and rectitude.

2. Much of the wisdom that made Maya civilization great lives on in the teaching and oral tradition of the elders. Unfortunately, not enough attention has been paid to the stories of indigenous people. Instead, they have been scorned or

rejected as the true heirs of the great civilization of their ancestors. This passage refers also to the grandeur of the Jakaltek Maya culture that was founded by B'alunh Q'ana' and Imox, the first Father and first Mother, founders of the town of Jacaltenango.

3. During the First Rain and Maya New Year ceremonies, the *alcaldes rezadores* (prayer makers) would burn *pom* (copal) and *k'ej ixkab'* (black beeswax) on the peak of Q'anil Mountain, which is also known as the "Volcano of War." Similarly, the elders would go to this sanctuary to burn candles when young men from the town were taken for military service. These rituals were suspended for several years, but now the *txahlom* (rezadores or prayer makers), who are trying to restore the strength of the Maya culture of the region, are again performing rain ceremonies on Mount Q'anil.

4. Xhuwan Q'anil (Juan Mendoza) and Xhuwan Mentes (Juan Méndez) are the two Jakaltek heroes who offered up their lives for their people. According to the legend, the two men received the power of the lightning and thus defeated the enemy. But because of having acquired supernatural powers, they were no longer able to live like normal people in their town, and therefore they went to live on the mountaintop, at the sanctuary of Q'anil. Every Jakaltek learns the legend of the Man of Lightning (Q'anil) as a child, and this gives the people a unique identity that unites them with their mythical and historical past. Jakalteks are also called *k'uh winaj* (Men of Lightning), because the legend says that a Man of Lightning exists in each and every Jakaltek.

5. Like all indigenous peoples of the continent, the Jakalteks have their legendary heroes who care for and defend their people. According to the elders, the Jakalteks have never died in distant wars and have always returned home after being called to the aid of their allies. According to the legend, it is for this reason that they were invited to aid the town that was in danger of being destroyed.

6. Having been banned from freely continuing the practice of Maya culture, the elders complain about the years that go by without their being able to fully recover their traditions and about the knowledge that is being lost. For example, the *ahb'e* (Maya diviners and calendar experts) have been accused of being witches and carriers of absurd knowledge or superstitions. Fortunately, there is now substantial interest in the revitalization of Maya culture in Guatemala.

7. The *clarinero (hoh ch'ok* or great-tailed grackle, *Cassidix mexicanus)* is a bird whose habitat is along riverbanks or near springs. When this bird sings with its beak pointing up toward the clouds, it is a signal that it is going to rain; therefore, according to Jakaltek belief, the bird is "asking for rain." This bird appears in the flood legends told by the Jakalteks.

8. From the Maya-Jakaltek language, *satkanh* (from *sat*, "face," and *kanh*, "God" or "sky") is a compound word that symbolizes the beauty of the sky (with the stars, sun, moon, and so forth). In other words, satkanh means "the beautiful face of God."

9. Among the first parents or group of ancestors who founded the town of Jacaltenango is B'alunh Q'ana', who was the oldest and wisest of seven brothers. Jakaltek legend tells that our first parents (B'alunh Q'ana' and Imox) retreated to the cave of Yula', where the Blue River has its source, to avoid being enslaved and baptized by the Spaniards during the Spanish invasion of the Cuchumatán Mountains in 1526.

10. The *xahanb'al* is a sacred offering to God. It is a type of mole (turkey with toasted, ground corn) that is offered to the divinity during a Maya religious ceremony. For example, the xahanb'al is made during the Maya New Year (Ijom Hab'il) or during the communal ceremony asking for rain. "Xahanb'al" means "to do or present something holy or sacred."

11. The original Maya name of Jacaltenango, "Xajla'" means "place of slabs and springs." Xajla' was also called Niman Konhob' (Large or Main Town). During the invasion, Xajla' was renamed Xacaltenango (Jacaltenango) by the Náhuatl-speaking Tlaxcaltecs who accompanied the Spaniards during the conquest of Guatemala.

One

12. B'alunh Q'ana' and Imox are the names of the first parents and founders of Xajla'. As mythical ancestors of the Jakalteks, B'alunh Q'ana' and Imox are also names of days on the Jakaltek Maya calendar.

13. According to Jakaltek oral tradition, corn and its different varieties were first discovered at K'unha Ch'en ("sacred house of stone" or "stone granary") in Jakaltek territory, near Q'anil Mountain.

14. The grandparents' teachings emphasize respect and communal unity of the people with nature and the supernatural.

15. The Maya ancestors made *caites* (*xanhab'*, or coarse leather sandals) from the skins of deer and other animals they hunted.

16. Maya weaving with the back-strap loom is a pre-Hispanic art that indigenous women have maintained over the centuries. This tradition has been especially promoted by Maya women, who contribute enormously to household income with the sale of their craft production.

17. The *achiote* (*hox*, or annatto) is a bush *(Bixa orellana)* from whose fruit a red dye is extracted. It also serves as an ingredient in cooking.

18. The Maya were the first to utilize the symbol of zero in their vigesimal numbering system. This is one of the greatest Maya advances of all antiquity.

19. Allegorical figure: corn and woman as origin and maintenance of life. *Posol* with cacao *(kakaw yal ixim)* was the drink usually distributed to participants during communal works of labor and religious events.

20. The Maya who were specialists in prophecy concerned themselves with understanding the movements of the heavenly bodies in order to predict the future. Some of their predictions based on astronomical calculations have stood the test of time—even the destruction brought by the Spanish conquest. The book of hieroglyphics called the *Dresden Codex* contains the astronomical calculations of the planet Venus *(Saj B'es)*.

Two

21. In this section the founding of Xajla' is recounted. This story is of great importance to those who study indigenous cultures, as it tells how the territories they now occupy were established. According to the legend of the founding, the Jakalteks have a direct relationship with the supernatural powers, especially the lightning (k'uh), because the founder of Jacaltenango was the first man of lightning, B'alunh Q'ana' *(b'alunh,* "nine," and *q'ana'* or *q'anab'al,* "fer-de-lance," a type of snake). In other words, lightning is of greater importance in Jakaltek culture, than in other Maya cultures of the region.

22. "May no one be left behind and may we all together move forward!" This is a predominant teaching in the *Popol Wuj.* The Maya have always insisted on unity and corporate survival.

23. This section tells of the destruction of the Maya Empire, as well as the dispersion of the peoples during antiquity. Of this scattering of the peoples it is said: "Immediately we dispersed throughout the mountains; then we all left, each tribe took its own path, each family followed theirs" (Recinos 1980:63). We cannot be sure what the cause of the dispersion of ancient Maya culture was, but several legends of destruction exist, such as floods and rain of turpentine *(q'ol),* which refers to volcanic eruptions. Life on earth, according to the Maya, follows a cycle of creation, destruction, and regeneration.

24. Ajul is a small village east of Jacaltenango.

25. Xajla' was renamed Xacaltenango (which in Náhuatl means "place of huts *[jacales]* surrounded by rock") by the Tlaxcaltecs, allies of the Spanish invaders.

26. Meste' is a small village northeast of Jacaltenango.

27. The legend of the founding of Xajla' is spectacular. Jakaltek territory was not

chosen by chance, but by divine design. *"Ha' tx'otx',"* they said. "This is the promised land." (A similar legend tells of the founding of Tenochtitlán by the Mexicans: The city was to be constructed where they found an eagle, devouring a serpent, upon a prickly pear cactus.)

28. After selecting the site for the founding of Xajla', B'alunh Q'ana' decided to surround the city with lightning bolts or "guardian angels" *(stanheomal jet)*. Juvenal Casaverde (1976) provides us with some of the names and locations of the lightning bolts around Jacaltenango.

Three

29. The Maya priests and seers who specialized in religious rituals always provided people with their "reading" or vision of the future of their people. In Jacaltenango, these seers and experts in the interpretation of the Maya calendar are called ahb'e, or "those who guide the way."

30. In ancient times, the roofs of the houses in indigenous communities were made of various types of straw. When someone in the community needed to build a home, the neighbors would gather and build it together. The symbol of the straw roof is used here to emphasize the unity and equanimity that existed in the communities.

31. The *wech* (in Spanish, *gato de monte*) is a variety of fox recognized as an animal of ill omen. The belief is that if the wech crosses a walker's path, this indicates bad luck or danger on the path.

32. The owl *(aq'b'al noq')* is a nocturnal bird whose song is the announcement of an imminent death in the village, according to belief.

33. All peoples have legends and stories that tell of their feats and triumphs in the past. This could be seen as an ethnocentric characteristic that all peoples of the world exhibit, but in indigenous communities where history has been maintained in an oral form, these legends have a particularly important function of strengthening the ethnic and historical foundations of the people.

Four

34. In the indigenous communities of the Cuchumatán Mountains, people were called to public meetings in the central plaza by the drum. This practice was of great importance for the maintenance of the sociopolitical structure of the communities, because in these meetings, called *"lahti'"* (from *lah,* "to level or equal-

ize," and *ti'*, "mouth," "judgments," or "speech"; thus, "to level or equalize judgments") the problems of the community were discussed and solutions or communal agreements were reached.

35. According to the legend, the Jakalteks participated in a war very far from their native land, but the place they went is unknown.

36. The enemy fought from the sea and used unknown weapons. Could this be an allusion to the armed resistance with which the indigenous people attempted to stop the Spanish invasion?

37. Indigenous people do not call themselves "the vanquished" because, as the legend expresses, the Maya people have always resisted and continue to resist the forces of domination that have repressed them from the days of the invasion of Guatemala in 1524 to the present.

Five

38. It is said that in ancient times there were men with supernatural powers and knowledge called *tz'ajan sk'ul*. Some were good-hearted *(k'ul sk'ul)* and protected their community from dangers, but others *(tx'oj sk'ul)* did their best to cause problems and illnesses for the people. There were several categories of people with supernatural powers, for example, the *txumlum*, or seers; the ahb'e, who were experts in the ancient Maya calendar; and the *Komam Komi'* (fathers and mothers of the people), who were like guardian angels. On the other hand were the *nawals* (sorcerers), who were the most feared because of their crimes and the harm they could cause ordinary people.

39. In the past, the nawals (sorcerers) had a great deal of influence in indigenous villages, because they were said to be familiar with the extraordinary and able to cause pestilence, illness, and even death to their enemies. Generally, those who possessed occult powers, like the nawals, were also braggarts.

40. According to Maya belief, when a person is born, in the mountains a companion animal or alter ego *(yijomal spixan)* is also born. This companion animal, or "spirit bearer," is also widely known in ethnographic descriptions as the *tonal*. The power or strength of the animal companion depends on the day of birth, according to the ancient Maya calendar. For example, people with special powers generally have a jaguar as their alter ego, while the yijomal spixan of weaker people might be a raccoon or opossum. If something happens to the animal companion, the person also suffers the same consequences. Generally, the animal companion of the nawals (sorcerers) is an evil or poisonous animal.

41. Matzwalil is the devil, the Evil One (from *matz*, "is not," and *walil*, "good").

42. This verse reiterates that each and every Jakaltek must return to his land of origin and not be lost from the rest, the sense of community.

43. There are several categories of knowledge, good and bad, depending on the strength *(swinajil)* of the day and time that one is born.

44. Those who possess supernatural powers are usually the most humble and helpful, according to tradition, whereas the sorcerers here represent some undesirable traits in the community, such as pride, selfishness, and cunning.

45. Because of the lack of beasts of burden in the communities, the Maya became accustomed to carrying heavy loads on their backs. In this way, those who conducted long-distance business hired their own *mozos,* or porters, to carry their merchandise from one town to another. This situation of using the Maya as burden carriers has been exploited by the Ladinos who act as authorities in some indigenous communities, especially when there was no means of transportation in the mountainous regions of the Cuchumatanes.

Six

46. Xhuwan's concern is not personal or individual, but communal. Despite the fact that the sorcerers personify vanity itself, Xhuwan is concerned for their safety and their safe return home.

47. *Sat B'ak'ul,* or abyss, refers to the crags or cliffs of stone formed by the Cuchumatán Mountains east of Jacaltenango.

48. The Blue River is known as *Ha' Saj Ha',* or "white river," and has its origin at the foot of this huge wall of stone (Sat B'ak'ul) where Jich Mam and Jich Mi' (also known as B'alunh Q'ana' and Imox) retreated to live in the cave of Yula', where they died, according to Jakaltek oral tradition.

49. Through prayer and penitence, Xhuwan manages to enter into communication and establish a dialogue with the guardian angels of the town. But here it becomes evident that the k'uh also have a hierarchy of power, and Xhuwan is directed to seek whichever is most appropriate to his human condition.

50. Kaje (from *kaj*, "red") is located west of the town and in this legend is associated with the color red (or dark purple). But according to the Maya glyphs associated with the four points of the compass, the west is black.

51. Saj Tanhnaj Oy, "extinguished white corner post," is located north of the city. The color white is associated with the north.

52. Here Yoq'ob' Hos, or "egg goiter," plays a joke on Xhuwan. In Popb'al Ti'

(Jakaltek) one says *"X'eltij ha woq'ob'"* ("Your goiter came out") if a joke is being played on someone.

53. Xhuwan insists on his own personal surrender and offering his life, if necessary, to save the life of his people.

54. Q'anil is located southwest of Jacaltenango, and the color associated with the south is yellow, "q'an," which suggests the name of "Q'anil," or "yellow power."

Seven

55. Despite having the powers of lightning, Xhuwan continues to be humble and helpful. And with the modesty characteristic of the Maya hero, Xhuwan demonstrates his abilities as a good "bearer," in the literal as well as the figurative sense of the word. Xhuwan bears the responsibility of protecting the conceited sorcerers and of saving his people from the war toward which they are headed.

56. According to Jakaltek belief, the truly wise and powerful must not be arrogant or boastful. Instead, they should conduct themselves with humility and have patience with braggarts, because those who talk the most are not necessarily the most knowledgeable or capable.

Eight

57. Tenb'al May is a place in the Cuchumatán Mountains where travelers often camped (from *tenb'al,* "to push or emphasize," and *may,* "spirit and courage"). The elders used to say, *"Ko tenakanoj hunoj ko may."* "Let's smoke a cigarette to give ourselves courage."

58. Juan Méndez is the other bearer, whose name in the Popb'al Ti' (Jakaltek) language is Xhuwan Mentes.

59. The number three is mythical and sacred and is related to the ritual of transfer of powers.

60. So it seems that what man performs is imperfect. The heroes work hard to hone their skills. In other words, nothing comes easy without temperance and strength of character. The *Popol Wuj* tells the story of creation, in which several attempts were made before the desired human being was achieved.

61. During their practice, the two men of lightning destroy several trees, but Xhuwan immediately decides to plant others in place of those that were felled. Here respect for nature is demonstrated, for they destroy out of necessity, but then they repair the damage in order to maintain the ecological equilibrium.

62. In the legend, extraordinary events are emphasized. For example, causing rain to fall from a clear blue sky is a supernatural act. This confirms the relationship of the guardian angel k'uh to the clouds, rain, and storms.

Nine

63. The dispute continues, and the quarrels among the sorcerers demonstrate the chaos in which they live. In this way, their personal arrogance and lust for power lead them to attribute to themselves powers they do not have.

64. The ahb'e are the Maya diviners and priests who prepare (metaphorically) the way or the path to follow during the year (calendar cycle). Here they represent the guides of the army of Xajla', which is heading toward an unfamiliar place. The ahb'e also know how to distinguish between good and evil, and they soon expose the vanity, lies, and deceit characteristic of the sorcerers.

65. The sea is far from the indigenous communities of the Cuchumatán region. In existing versions of the legend, the name of the place where they went is not mentioned. Perhaps the name and place have been forgotten over time. But in the *Annals of the Kaqchikels* we read the following: "Then we arrived at the seashore. There on the shore all the tribes and warriors were gathered. And when they contemplated it, their hearts were oppressed. 'There is no way to get across; we have not known of anyone who has crossed the sea'" (Recinos 1980:57–58).

66. The sorcerers, when transformed into their tonales or yijomal spixan (alter egos), were capable of causing panic among simple townspeople. So it is that the sorcerers are defeated by their own naïveté, because they had not considered the danger their lives could be in. The sorcerers' occult powers are useless in a war in which the weapons are different from those normally encountered. (The legend says "strange weapons." Could these be the firearms used during the Spanish Conquest?) In this way, the sorcerers fail again, because they are unaware of the magnitude of the problem into which they have gotten themselves.

67. Xhuwan had foreseen the premature defeat of the sorcerers and therefore had prepared himself in order to avoid discrediting his people. In other words, Xhuwan was the only one who had prepared himself with Maya rituals before leaving his town, because he knew the importance of defeating an enemy that fought with more powerful weapons.

68. As was to be expected, the humble image of the campesinos (peasants) inspires disappointment. According to the reputation of the warriors of Xajla', they should present themselves as ferocious and extraordinary warriors; instead,

the bearers of Xajla' present themselves humbly, hiding their power and their secret.

69. Here arises the problem of communication between members of different linguistic groups that come into contact. Generally, indigenous people speak the languages of the neighboring towns with which they have the most contact and socioeconomic relationships. But the farther away the populations are, the less they know of each other's customs and languages, even though they belong to the same culture and speak languages with a common Maya base or origin.

Ten

70. The legend tells that these invaders fought from the sea, hidden under the waves. Many of the first battles between the Spaniards and the indigenous people took place on the coast, when the Spaniards came ashore. For example, Bernal Díaz del Castillo mentions Cortés's arrival on the coast of Tabasco in this way: "With their drums, they gave the signal for a general attack to surround us, while they shot arrows at us. Then they surrounded us with their canoes and then we were forced to fight them, with our bodies in the water" (Díaz del Castillo 1927:69).

71. The presence and participation of the brother from Chiapas in this mission demonstrates the friendship and brotherhood that existed between Maya on both sides of the Guatemalan-Mexican border. The ability to arrive quickly on the scene and give aid to those in need is also a characteristic of the Komam Komi', "Fathers and Mothers," or guardian angels of the people.

72. Some elders say that the apprentice, Xhuwan Mentes (Juan Méndez), acted first, stirring up the waters and thereby revealing the enemy.

73. The waters of the sea were red with the blood of those who died in the battle. Some accounts of the massacres committed during the Spanish invasion recount situations similar to this. In Alvarado's battle with the K'iche' on the plains of Quetzaltenango, it is stated that "countless barbarians died there, so that for a long time the river of that meadow was turned into blood" (*Isagoge histórica apologética de las Indias Occidentales* 1935:185).

74. In this section a telescopic time process is used (recalling a distant event and inserting it into this more recent story). Thus, it seems that an allusion is being made to the war of the Spaniards against the Moors, because even the elders believe that the reference to the manufacturers of beautiful silks refers to the Turks.

75. Oxlanh B'en (Oxlanh, "thirteen," and B'en, one of the twenty day names

according to the Maya calendar) is considered here to be a prophetic number. B'en is also a day of bad luck according to the *Chilam Balam of Tizimín* (Edmonson 1982, Makemson 1951). It could also refer to the end of the millennium at Oxlanh B'ak'tun.

76. The warriors of Xajla' did not desire power or riches. They came only to aid an oppressed people. After fighting to liberate them, they returned home, declining the honors and tribute that were offered them.

Eleven

77. As explained above, the legend has interwoven different historical facts important to the Jakalteks. It is not known how they crossed the sea and arrived on the scene, but by means of comparison, we present an excerpt from the *Annals of the Kaqchikels,* which states how they crossed the sea: "We thrust the point of our walking sticks into the sand under the sea and we soon crossed the sea over the sand. . . . In this way we passed over the sands lined up, when the depths of the sea and the surface of the sea had been widened. They threw themselves then and passed over the sand; those who were coming last were entering the sea when we were coming ashore on the other side of the waters" (Recinos 1980:58–59).

78. The two men of lightning fulfill their promise of not returning to their home, for because of their having shared supernatural powers, they are no longer common campesinos like the others. They have achieved a status superior to that of humans, and therefore they must live in isolation in order to continue their mission as guardians and protectors of the people.

79. When there is thunder and lightning, it is said that the k'uh are patrolling the sky and preventing dangers and catastrophes that could destroy the town. Some elders say that due to the lightning's action, the hail falls in small pieces and not in huge blocks that could destroy the crops.

80. The cycle of the legendary hero is complete: his departure, his triumph over tribulations, and finally his return to the land of his origin.

81. Many of the Jakaltek legends are shared with the Maya peoples of Chiapas, especially the Tojolabals, Tzotzils, and Tzeltals. The name "Juan Carmelo" has been Mayanized as "Xhuwan Kalmel."

82. The two bearers who became men of lightning took up residence in the sanctuary of Q'anil, which symbolizes the personification of the ancestors in hills and volcanoes, always present and eternal in the eyes of their descendants.

83. Having remained in the oral tradition for several centuries, although frag-

mentarily, the legend of Xhuwan Q'anil persists to the present day. Unfortunately, the legend has lost much of its force as a symbol of identity for the Jakalteks. Therefore, recreating and transferring this epic poem from the oral tradition to a written text is an attempt to highlight the moral and cultural values represented in this legend by the Jakaltek hero, Xhuwan Q'anil.

Bibliography

Anonymous

1935   *Isagoge histórica apologética de las Indias Occidentales y especial de la Provincia de San Vicente de Chiapa y Guatemala,* vol. 8. Guatemala: Biblioteca "Goathemala" de la Sociedad de Geografía e Historia.

Bassie-Sweet, Karen

1991   *From the Mouth of the Dark Cave.* Norman: University of Oklahoma Press.

Bricker, Victoria R.

1981   *The Indian Christ, the Indian King: The Historical Substrate of Maya Myth and Ritual.* Austin: University of Texas Press.

Carmack, Robert M., and James L. Mondloch, trans.

1989   *El Título de Yax y otros documentos quichés de Totonicapán, Guatemala.* México: Universidad Nacional Autónoma de México.

Casaverde, Juvenal R.

1976   *Jacaltec Social and Political Structure.* Ann Arbor, Mich.: University Microfilms.

Colby, Benjamin N., and Lore M. Colby

1981   *The Daykeeper: The Life and Discourse of an Ixil Diviner.* Cambridge: Harvard University Press.

Columbus, Christopher

1988   *The Four Voyages of Columbus,* trans. Cecil Jane. New York: Dover.

Cox de Collins, Anne

1980   *Colonial Jacaltenango, Guatemala: The Formation of a Corporate Community.* Ann Arbor, Mich.: University Microfilms.

Craine, E. R., and R. C. Reindorp, eds. and trans.

1979   *The Codex Pérez and the Book of Chilam Balam of Maní.* Norman: University of Oklahoma Press.

Díaz del Castillo, Bernal

1927   *The True History of the Conquest of Mexico,* vol. 1. New York: Robert McBride and Company.

Edmonson, Munro S.

1982   *The Ancient Future of Itza: The Book of Chilam Balam of Tizimín.* Austin, University of Texas Press.

Estrada Monroy, Agustín

1985   "Título de Jacaltenango," in *Anales de la Academia de Geografía e Historia de Guatemala,* tomo LIX, año LXI. Guatemala: Editorial José de Pineda Ibarra.

Fuentes y Guzmán, F. A.

1969–72   "Recordación Florida," in *Obras históricas de Don Francisco Antonio de Fuentes y Guzmán,* 3 vols. Madrid: Biblioteca de Autores Españoles.

Gall, Francis

1963   *Título de los de León y Cardona,* publicación no. 11. Guatemala: Centro Editorial "José de Pineda Ibarra."

Goetz, Delia, and Sylvanus Morley, trans.

1983   *Popol Vuh: The Sacred Book of the Ancient Quiché Maya.* Norman: University of Oklahoma Press.

Gossen, Gary H.

1984   *Chamulas in the World of the Sun: Time and Space in a Maya Oral Tradition.* Prospect Heights, Ill.: Waveland Press.

Kelley, David H.

1976   *Deciphering the Maya Script.* Austin: University of Texas Press.

La Farge, Oliver

1947   *Santa Eulalia: The Religion of a Cuchumatán Indian Town.* Chicago: University of Chicago Press.

———, and Douglas Byers

1931   *The Year Bearer's People.* New Orleans: Middle American Research Institute, Tulane University.

1994   *La costumbre en Santa Eulalia, Huehuetenango en 1932.* California: Yax Te' Press.

1997   *El Pueblo de los cargadores del año,* trans. Oscar Velázquez and Víctor Montejo. California: Yax Te' Press.

Landa, Diego de

1983   *Relación de las cosas de Yucatán.* Mérida: Ediciones Dante.

Laughlin, Robert M.

1988   *The People of the Bat: Mayan Tales and Dreams from Zinacantan,* ed. Carol Karasik. Washington, D.C.: Smithsonian Institution Press.

Lomelí González, Arturo

1988   *Algunas costumbres y tradiciones del mundo tojolabal.* San Cristóbal de las Casas, Chiapas: Dirección de Fortalecimiento y Fomento a las Culturas.

Lovell, W. George

1985   *Conquest and Survival in Colonial Guatemala: A Historical Geography of the Chuchumatán Highlands, 1500–1821.* Kingstone and Montreal: McGill-Queen's University Press.

1992a   "Los registros parroquiales de Jacaltenango, Guatemala," in *Mesoamérica,* CIRMA, Antigua Guatemala, Año 13, no. 24, pp. 441–53.

1992b   *Conquista y cambio cultural: La Sierra de los Cuchumatanes de Guatemala, 1500–1821,* Serie Monográfica no. 6. Antigua: CIRMA; South Woodstock, Vt.: Plumsock Mesoamerican Studies.

Makemson, Maud W.

1951   *The Book of the Jaguar Priest, a Translation of the Book of Chilam Balam of Tizimín.* New York: Henry Schuman.

Montejo, Victor D.

1984   *El Kanil: Man of Lightning.* Carrboro, N.C.: Signal Books.

1991   *The Bird Who Cleans the World, and Other Mayan Fables.* Willimantic, Conn.: Curbstone Press.

Oakes, Maude

1951   *The Two Crosses of Todos Santos: Survivals of Mayan Rituals.* New York: Pantheon Books, Inc.

Pickands, Martin

1986   "The Hero Myth in Maya Folklore," in *Symbol and Meaning Beyond the Closed Community: Essays in Mesoamerican Ideas,* ed. Gary H. Gossen. Albany, N.Y.: State University of New York Institute for Mesoamerican Studies, pp. 101–03.

Recinos, Adrián, trans.

1978   *El Popol Vuj: Las antiguas historias del Quiché.* San José, Costa Rica: Editorial Americana.

1980   *Memorial de Sololá (Memorial de Tecpán-Atitlán), Anales de los cakchiqueles y Título de los Señores de Totonicapán,* Biblioteca Americana, Serie Literatura Indígena. México: Fondo de Cultura Económica.

1983   *Crónicas indígenas de Guatemala,* 2a ed. Guatemala: Academia de Geografía e Historia.

Roys, Ralph L.

1967   *The Book of Chilam Balam of Chumayel.* Norman: University of Oklahoma Press.

Shaw, Mary, ed.

1971   *According to our Ancestors: Folk Texts from Guatemala and Honduras.* Guatemala: Summer Institute of Linguistics.

Spero, Joanne M.

1987   *Lightning Men and Water Serpents: A Comparison of Mayan and Mixe-Zoquean Beliefs.* M.A. Thesis, Department of Anthropology, University of Texas at Austin.

Tedlock, Dennis, trans.

1996   *Popol Vuj: The Mayan Book of the Dawn of Life,* rev. ed. New York: Simon & Schuster.

About the Author

Víctor Montejo is a distinguished Maya anthropologist and author who had to leave Guatemala during the early eighties. He obtained his Ph.D. in anthropology from the University of Connecticut in 1993. Dr. Montejo has taught at Bucknell University and the University of Montana in Missoula; currently, he is Associate Professor and Chair of the Native American Studies Department at the University of California, Davis. He is the author of several books, including *Testimony: Death of a Guatemalan Village; The Bird Who Cleans the World and Other Mayan Fables; Sculpted Stones* (Curbstone Press); *Las aventuras de Mister Puttison entre los mayas; Q'anil, el hombre rayo/Komam Q'anil, ya' k'uh winaj* (Yax Te' Foundation); *Voices from Exile: Violence and Survival in Modern Maya History* (University of Oklahoma Press); and *Popol Vuh: A Sacred Book of the Maya* (a version for young readers) (Groundwood Books, Ontario, Canada).